FIJI: Journey to the South Pacific

By

Dorothy J. Ram

5-16-2011

Dear Shipra & Shanti:

Thank you for having us over when Maiana & Michael where in S.F. Enjoyed the brunch and the gathering and the talking. Whoever mixed a mamosa for me did a good job - it knocked me out! Way to go Aaron! I love being around you people, I get good feelings.

All the Best,
Rosie

Shanti - you make the best Wine Coolers!

FIJI: Journey to the South Pacific

Author: Ram, Dorothy J.

Publisher: Lulu

Date of Publication:

ISBN: 978-0-557-02887-0

4-11-11

Dear Shipra enjoy
2 hope you this .
reading all the best
Dorothy

DEDICATION

This book is dedicated to my Husband, for his patience while I adjusted to a whole new world.

To my husband Claudius,
Who on our Wedding Day promised,
"I'll take you to places that you've never been". You certainly did that, my husband, my friend.

To my children: Deborah, Richard, and Diane, who put up with me when I was slightly crazy being a mother, wife, and my own person, while trying to learn the language, life, and ways of Fiji. To my daughter-in-law, Cheryl who brought with her so much talent, love and support when she came into our family. I would have been lost many times with out her.

To my grandchildren: Shaun, Christopher, Nathan, Rebecca, and Kajah, who bring me such joy as I watch them shift so easily from one world to another, enjoying the process as they go.

Acknowledgements

Without the help of these people this book would not have come into being: my daughters, Deborah and Diane, who edited so beautifully; Rosemarie Williams, who read and asked many questions; David Brown, who kept encouraging me when I faltered; my beautiful and only granddaughter Rebecca and my first-born grandson, Shaun, who assisted with the graphics and formatting. For all their help, I am very grateful.

Cover picture:
Commissioned artwork done by Fred Whippy,
Fiji 1975.

Cover design by: Diane Ram and Megan Runneals

ABOUT THE AUTHOR

By Diane Ram and David Brown

Dorothy Williams was born to Harold Williams, a farmer of Ohio and Evelyn Rogers, a socialite of Indiana in August of 1935. Dorothy is one of seven children. She met her husband, Claudius Ram (Richard) in 1953 while in her senior year at Huntington High School and they married three months later.

They lived in the US from 1954 to 1960, until Claudius was called home to Fiji to help in the family timber business. With two toddlers, Deborah age 4, and Richard, at 18 months, they journeyed to a small village off the Coral Coast called Navutulevu. This is where her extraordinary story of life in Fiji begins.

Excerpted from May 13, 2009 Pacifica Tribune article

From Midwest farm to far away island, Dorothy Ram writes of adventure and love
By Jean Bartlett
Pacifica Tribune Arts Correspondent

Fifty-five years ago, Midwestern-born farm girl Dorothy Ram fell for the young man from Fiji whose car broke down in her hometown of Chillicothe, Ohio – and now, she has written an autobiography.

Ram was a senior in high school when she met Claudius. He went by Richard then. He had left Fiji on a working ship when he was 21 and jumped ship with a friend (due essentially to being 21 and ready to have adventures) in Vancouver, Washington. He changed his name to Richard and headed off to work and travel. It is another story, not yet written down, how Claudius came to arrive in Chillicothe, but the fact that he and Dorothy met almost seems destined by the stars.

"The strange thing about it is my husband's ancestors came to Fiji on a ship and their journey started from Chillicothe, Ohio," said Ram. "My mother-in-law's grandfather was a man named Moses Work. And according to the local historian Beverly Gray, there was a Moses Work who had a hardware store on the main street in Chillicothe. This Moses Work purchased a ship in Virginia and from there sailed to the South Pacific. It does seem "full circle" that Claudius would accidentally stop in the hometown of Mr. Work."

Married three months after they met, the couple stayed in the Midwest until seven years into their marriage when Claudius answered his father's call to come home and help with the family's logging business.

"You couldn't have been more "country" than me," laughed Ram. "I didn't know anything other than the Midwest. My family was farmers through and through. We milked cows for a living, slopped the hogs, got the hay in. I liked growing up in Ohio. I was in the 4-H club from childhood right up until my engagement."

The first time Ram saw the ocean was on her way to her new life in Fiji. She admitted because she didn't know what life would be like in Fiji, she just plunged right in. This book "Fiji: My Journey to the South Pacific," introduces the reader, like the young girl from the Midwest, into a world far away from Chillicothe, Ohio.

Dorothy made lifetime friendships in Fiji and said, as is evidenced in her book, that the people are charming and loving. "With the Fijian women, their whole world revolved around the family, gathering the food and the wood, what to plant - and I miss that camaraderie." At the same time, Dorothy missed the mental stimulation from home comforts such as: "the newspaper, the television and magazines."

At 147 double-spaced pages, Ram's book quite simply cannot tell all. But what she does tell in her book is crisp, frank, observant and visual, always with a strong love story, talked about or not, that anchors her feet to strength and earth and adventure.

"Fiji: My Journey to the South Pacific," is the kind of story that stays with you; that enters your dreams as easily as the author's descriptions of Fiji fall from page into mind. Dorothy writes there are, "No streetlights (that) illuminate this corner of the world. (Instead) a glowing cruise liner passes by like a fairy ship in the night" or "a warm (moon) glow illuminates everything (including) the ripples on the water sparkling like diamonds along a silvery path."

Dorothy Ram has a strong literary voice and with it, she reaches out across the water to reveal a young pioneer-like woman, who would find from her island perch a view from left to right of: "Ocean and sky and islands out in the ocean and fish jumping. A view that was perhaps the most calming and beautiful thing that I have ever experienced."

Award-winning journalist and children's book author, Jean Bartlett is the Arts Correspondent for the Pacifica Tribune. Additionally a "private" biographer, Ms. Bartlett can be contacted through her website: editor@jeansmagazines.org.

TABLE OF CONTENTS

Chapter One

Fiji Islands January 20, 1960

BACK IN TIME

I was twenty-five years old when my journey to Fiji began. I remember that day, more than forty-five years ago, as if it were only yesterday. It was the day our big silver plane circled over the lush green islands, hugged by beautiful hues of water, some aqua-green, some deep blue, and the white of the breakers dashing against the reef. We set down on Fiji soil and I leaned over in my seat to get a better look out of the window and eagerly wondered what was in store for us here in this part of the world that was completely unknown to me. My husband, Richard (known in Fiji as Claudius,) and I had been married for six years living and working in northern Illinois with our two small children when his family asked him to come home to Fiji to work in the family's timber business.

The Boeing 707 left Chicago, Illinois, on January 11th, 1960, in a swirling snowstorm. Our first stop was San Francisco, California, where we changed planes.

Then on to Honolulu, Hawaii to refuel, and then on to another refueling stop on Canton Island, a small spit of land in the middle of the Pacific Ocean. A tall, stately Fijian served us sandwiches and soft drinks. Incredibly, Richard and he knew each other and there were grins all around as the other passengers watched them get reacquainted. Taking off from Canton Island involved starting at the edge of the water on one side of the island and pulling the nose up sharply as the runway met the ocean at the other end of the island, leaving no part of the runway unused. Not an experience I would care to repeat.

I was born and raised in the foothills of the Appalachian Mountains in Southern Ohio. There, I met my husband. My Uncle Earl warned me before I left Ohio for Fiji that I'd be "living in a tree house and wearing grass skirts." Uncle Earl was my mother's stepbrother, a very kind but opinionated man. He and his wife were childless so he involved himself in our lives, always sending money for birthdays and Christmas and visiting whenever he could. Uncle Earl, was born of a mixed race couple, and had married a white woman. He immersed himself in that world by passing for white. In this way he managed to get into a great career as an advertising artist.

He designed labels for Campbell's Soup and other companies, often walking a fine line between two worlds, colored and white. He loved us and we knew it. Mom regaled us often about his exploits as a child growing up. It is a wonder he finished his formal education given all the schools he was kicked out of.

My destination must have caused him great concern given the circumstances he perceived that I would be living under. Not knowing the first thing about the South Pacific, I had little doubt that what he had said was true. As the plane circled the Island, I caught sight of lovely little multi-colored houses nestled among the palm trees. I breathed a sigh of relief thinking that at least some people lived in houses here.

Getting off the plane in Nadi was like walking into a steam room. While my husband was going through customs, I had time to look about the terminal and noticed people staring at my children and me. It did not take me long to realize we were the object of very animated conversation. My son Ricky, who was 18 months, and my daughter Debbie, who was 4½, were tired and worn out from the nearly twenty-two hours of flying, but Fijians loved babies and Ricky's chubby legs drew many an admiring smile. Later, I found out that the real reason was that most of these people knew Richard.

My husband left Fiji in December of 1951, when he was 21 years old. At that time, he worked as an engineer for Bish Limited in Suva. He was then offered a job on the ship, Lakeba. The Lakeba sailed from Suva to Vancouver, British Columbia, and down the Oregon coast to Vancouver, Washington. When he reached Vancouver, Washington, Richard and his friend Vincent Grant decided to leave the ship and stay in the United States. They each put on three sets of clothes – shirts, trousers, and socks. Leaving the rest of their belongings behind, they left the ship. The ship's Captain as standard procedure to prevent illegal entry into the United States kept their passports, but that did not stop them. They caught a bus from Vancouver, Washington, to Portland, Oregon, and a midnight train to Seattle, Washington. In Seattle, they changed their names. Claudius Ram became Richard Saunders, and Vincent Grant became John Ceretti. Thus, began an adventure that would completely change their lives. How Richard ended up in Southern Ohio is another story. But now, nine years later, he was home with his American wife and children.

Back in the airport, a beaming taxi driver led us to his waiting cab. After we were all installed, he sped out of the airport taking the highway that led to Nadi town. This was the first time Richard had been home in nine years and his Fijian was rather rusty at first, but he was soon conversing away with the driver, presumably catching up on some local events that had happened during his absence. We drove through the town, which, at that time, was no more than a few sparse shops, not the thriving city that exists there today. The weather was very hot. Through the open window of the taxi, I could see miles and miles of sugar cane fields planted as far as the eye could see. Blue mountaintops rose above the haze of the horizon. The first sari clad Indian women we saw caused quite a stir in me. I thought the Indian women were so elegant and feminine, and the colors so lovely and gay, even though some of the saris were bright pink, chartreuse, and bright red. The colors in Fiji are very brilliant.

Soon we were approaching the Sigatoka Valley, which presented yet another picture of the landscape. The fields were getting greener and the road ran along the beaches and through the villages with houses made of matted bamboo with thatched roofs. We had sent Richard's family a telegram telling them of our arrival, but neither my husband nor the driver seemed very concerned that no one was at the airport to meet us. Even though the telegram had been sent four days earlier, the driver assured us that it had not had time to reach them. That was my first realization that time in these Fiji Islands was meant to be taken very slowly. "*Vaka-malua*" as the Fijians say, which simply means unhurried, or even a little sedate and tranquil. Westerners coming to these shores who ignore this law soon find themselves chasing their own tails, including me.

Another unforgettable sight that day was of a European man walking completely nude on the beach as if to say that he had come to these islands to get away from it all, and he intended to do just that. I'm happy to say that that was the last time I saw such a sight. Although the teeny bikinis leave much to be desired, they are a great improvement on nature alone!

As we entered Richard's home region, where he was born and raised and where he had gone to school, he began noticing familiar faces and calling out names. I glanced back through the rear window. They stood bewildered for a moment, then a grin would surface and soon a wave of recognition would flood their faces as they realized that it was "Claudius" returned home from America. At one point Richard excitedly stuck his head out of the car window and yelled, "Nine-and-a half!" His friend had been given that name in school because half of a finger was missing. I spotted Nine-and-a half grinning broadly in the dust of the road. Initially, I was shocked at the insult and wondered why he would address his friend in this manner. Later, I realized these were pet names that they often used fondly for each other.

Another good friend of his was Cat's-Eye, due to his glass eye. For weeks I called another very nice man "*Matava*" and another "*Cobi*", (pronounced Thomby), until I found out these names meant "Four-eyes" and "Baldy".

I began to realize why we had been the objects of such animated conversation at the airport. It seemed that my husband knew practically everyone on the Island and almost everyone knew him. They knew that he had gone off on a ship some years ago, and had left the ship to start a new life in America. Now he was home with his American wife, daughter, and baby son. His home was about to become mine.

Chapter Two

January 1960 – May 1960

NADRIYALEWA

Just before reaching Navutulevu Village, we turned left by the bridge, off of the main highway, known as the Queens Road. We drove through rows of banana trees, patches of green dalo plants and followed the creek for about a mile and a half to an area known as Nadriyalewa. The taxi drew up at the head of a row of rough weatherboard houses. I remember thinking "Why are we stopping here?" Everyone started to pile out of the car, including my husband, so I thought, "Maybe I'd better get out, too". The houses seemed completely surrounded by dense foliage and tall trees. The only bright spot was the creek that was babbling merrily along by the side of the houses creating a tinkling sound as it went on its way. Looking around, I thought "What a dreary depressing place to live". Soon people surrounded us. People my husband had not seen for nine years. He himself had not known what to expect as when he had left for America his family had been living in the city of Suva, the capital of Fiji, fifty miles away. Suva was a modern bustling city. The whole family had now relocated into the middle of the tropical bush.

Dad, (Richard's father, Raja Ram) had set up a timber company in 1947 with his partners. After a couple of years he bought his partners out and continued the business with his son, Wallace. The family moved to Navutulevu and set up the new mill in this location in 1951. They started with two pair of bullocks, #1 and #2 chain saws, and a 25 horsepower gasoline engine with two flywheels. About that time, Claudius got the chance to work on the ship. He left and his family operated the mill with the help of Fijian and Indian laborers. When Dad's youngest son was out of school he joined the family in the mill and Dad saw the opportunity to expand his operation. Dad moved the mill another half mile inland, enlarged it, added a D4 tractor and bought trucks to haul the timber. He continued to hire more people. At that time, he had about twenty men working for him. In later years, Dad was appointed to the Fiji Forestry Board. It was from that small beginning in Nadriyalewa that Dad developed his company into one of the largest timber businesses in Fiji. He was awarded the honor of OBE, Order of the British Empire, awarded for services rendered to the United Kingdom and its people. Fiji at that time was a Crown Colony obtaining their independence from England in October 1970. Sadly, Dad did not live long enough to see his medal. It was delivered posthumously, because Dad died of a heart attack December the 8th that very same year while preparing for a trip to India. The other members of his India tour group stopped by the house on their way to the airport to pay their respects. The day of Dad's funeral services, the plane carrying his tour group to India flew low over the cemetery dipping a wing as they flew out to sea.

As our taxi was unloaded, I stood in the middle of the compound. The housing consisted of small wooden homes, one for Dad and Ma, (Richard's mother, Esther) set back on a little rise, one for Wallace and his wife Kini and, another for Lella, (Richard's sister) and her husband Jangu Singh. Another house was built for us and a long row of smaller homes further away housed the laborers and their families. It finally dawned on me, so this is where we are going to live! When I looked up, I caught Richard looking at me with such a look of tender compassion that I knew he must have been thinking, "How is she going to take all of this?"

Faces started to emerge, first a medium built slender girl, maybe an inch taller than my five feet two, with black hair and smooth almond skin and, a trace of Chinese features. This, I thought, must be Kini, married to Richard's older brother, Wallace. Tears came to her eyes and she kissed Richard lightly on the cheek, extended her hand and kissed me, and looked with love and tenderness on Debbie and Ricky. Next, came Lella, an exotic looking girl even shorter than me, with small features, a flawless complexion, almond shaped eyes, and the most beautiful hair I had ever seen. It glistened blue black and hung well below her hips. She too had tears in her eyes for this brother of hers that she had not seen in such a long time. Richard embraced his only sister, and I remember thinking how well controlled these people are. My family would have been loud, bear hugging, and shedding buckets of tears at such a reunion. The children were running around with so many little tots, some belonged to the laborers. They were running around laughing and adding to my confusion of so many strange people.

Ma's house consisted of two rooms. One for sleeping and a smaller sitting room with four canvas chairs clustered around a low coffee table on which sat a radio and a vase of flowers. In another corner was a single bed tucked away behind a curtain. The sleeping room held four large double beds and a wardrobe. Walking on through to the back door about ten feet from the house was an outside kitchen. The most dismal kitchen I believe I have ever seen. It consisted of two sections. In the front section was a long table with two long benches running down either side. Behind a partition was an old wooden cook stove. I had not seen a stove like that, except at my Grandmother's house, for many long years. Looking through the door outside, I could see wooden shelves nailed up along the wall holding tin plates, glasses, pots and silverware all drying in the sun.

The only work counter was a high shelf, almost waist high about three feet long and seemingly used for preparing food. I thought about my bright, shiny kitchen in Chicago, the gleaming chrome of the dinette set, the white stove and shiny silver knobs and buttons, the stainless steel double sinks, the cupboards crammed with every conceivable item to make a woman's work easier. I had walked out of the future into the past and, for the first time on that long journey, I regretted having left home.

In this kitchen, Mom, Kini and some women helpers did the cooking that was served cafeteria style. First, the men were fed at the long wooden table, then the children, and last of all, the women sat down to have their meal. It was beyond me how anyone prepared a meal in that kitchen, but they did with no refrigerator, no work table, very few utensils and the need to build a fire in the wooden stove. I marveled at their ability to feed so many people such delicious meals. I thought, at that time and still do, that his mother was probably one of the best cooks I have ever encountered. Every meal she put out was delicious.

I walked out of the house and looked up at the sky. It had begun to drizzle and a little yellow-breasted bird had taken refuge under a coconut frond and had begun to sing. I listened to its song for a moment then turned my attention to a partially completed structure, sitting about five feet away. It was a little larger than Ma's house and seemed cool and airy. One of the children told me that it was to be our house. In the meantime, we would be sleeping in Lella's house, the small house closest to the little creek. About this time a car drove up. It proved to be Richard's parents who, after receiving our telegram that very day, had gone off to investigate the whereabouts of their middle son.

Mom was slight, small and, barely five feet with thick brown hair mixed with grey. She was of Fijian and European descent. Her face was imprinted by the years and one could tell at a glance that she knew what hard work was. She ignored Richard and I completely but gathered her grandchildren in her arms and sat on the floor sobbing and swaying back and forth crooning words of endearment to these children of her son whom she had all but given up hope of ever seeing again. When Claudius Ram had walked off the ship in Vancouver, Washington, he had assumed a new identity and become Richard Saunders. Even though they had not seen their son in almost ten years, everyone called him Richard as a courtesy to the children and me since they knew it was the only name we had ever called him by. It was a courtesy that I never forgot.

My father-in-law, Raja, was short, heavy set with black hair, medium complexion and fine chiseled features. He was a Hindu. I saw in him a reflection of my own husband. Although Richard was taller, fairer and slimmer, the resemblance between father and son was there to see. He extended his hand to both of us, patted his grandchildren on their heads, and asked if we had had our tea. This was my first introduction to the proverbial tea, which can mean breakfast, lunch or dinner. It also meant ten o'clock and four o'clock tea. Lella married a tall handsome Nepali man by the name of Jang Bahadur Singh. I always loved that name and I loved Jangu. He was one of the kindest, sweetest persons that I met in Fiji. From the first time we met, until twenty years later when he died suddenly at work from a heart attack, he was always the same kind, smiling person.

Jangu had been previously married in an arranged marriage. But his only love was Lella. Lella had almond brown eyes and raven black hair reaching down to her waist. This love caused a rift in Jangu's family and they never really accepted Lella as part of their family. She wasn't of their choosing. Lella and Jangu never had children of their own, and Lella seemed to think that it was a curse put upon her by his family. Whether that was true or not, Lella and Jangu loved each other 'till the day he died. When one of the workers came to the house to tell Lella that Jangu had had a heart attack and died, Lella drew back her fist and knocked the man down. She could not explain why she did it.

We spent that first night in Lella's house. She had added curtains and floor coverings and spreads to the beds. A decidedly feminine touch prevailed throughout the rooms. Richard tucked Debbie and Ricky into their mosquito nets, tucked ours in around us and climbed into bed beside me. The bed was very hard to me but the sheets and mosquito net smelled fresh and clean. The creek tinkled merrily away under the window. Richard reached over and pulled me into his arms and held me tightly. I finally let go of the tears and cried myself to sleep.

We quickly settled into life at the sawmill. Richard went off each morning to work. Our first house was completed and we moved in. We purchased living room and bedroom furniture. The mill carpenter made us a table and chairs for the kitchen, and I learned to cook on a Primus; a one burner kerosene stove with short legs, similar to a Coleman stove of today. We were honored by the building of a shower, and septic tank toilet made especially for us. But since it was the only shower there, everyone used it. Often times, you found yourself standing in line for the use of your own shower.

The Maytag gasoline motor washing machine finally arrived. We had ordered it before we left the States. It was quite an enlightenment to the family women who had been washing in the creek for so long. We told them to bring their clothes and wash whenever they felt like it. Kini had several children by that time and would pop in often. Next came Ma and Lella and, by the time I did my washing, the Maytag was running every day for most of the morning. I had no worries about it because I had faith in Maytag's. But one day it did give up the ghost temporarily. It was then that I found out what it was like to have to stoop down on my haunches in the creek with a flat board and a scrubbing brush and a piece of soap, to wash clothes.

Having never had the creek washing experience before, I can tell you that for a while my washing looked better before it was washed than after I finished washing it. Women there took great pride in their clean, white wash. All the socks were hung together, the shirts all hung by the seams. I didn't realize until later that the family women took my creek washed clothes from my clothes line, rewashed it and hung it again, all without a word to me. It was yet, another kindness that I will remember. I soon found out that the trick to clean clothes was to soak them all night in Rinso, boil them in hot water the next morning, and then finally scrub them. Boiling clothes was a new experience too. I had usually relied on a bottle of Clorox whenever I went to the laundry mat.

It was about this time that I had my first experience with the "devils" or "*tevoros*", as they are known in Fiji. Richard, his mother and father and I had gone up the creek for a good distance to try and catch some prawns. I donned shorts and canvas shoes and started off in high spirits. We caught a good bit and I started back. Since they were busy still catching prawns I decided to start back home on my own. It was a very refreshing walk through the clear creek bordered on both sides by dense undergrowth and trees. There was hardly any chance of getting lost as the creek ran right past the mill compound. Eventually, I reached home.

About a week later, I began to get a rash on both ankles that spread rapidly and set up a terrible itch. We did not have a car at the time. There was one car that was used by everyone in the family, so it was rarely available. The family assured Richard that my rash was nothing and could be cured easily by having an old lady come and massage my legs with oil, both morning and evening. Since this had no effect, except to make my legs worse, the *vuniwai* (doctor) was sent for. He was the Fijian Medical Officer in charge of several small medical dispensaries scattered through the island. He came and gave me a penicillin shot. In fact, he gave me several shots over the course of his visits. This still had no effect on me, and the family was now convinced that I had fallen under the spell of a *draunikau* (an evil spell) placed on me by tevoros (evil spirits) who saw me pass by in the creek that day all alone, and took a liking to me in my shorts, which are never worn by local women.

The rash was horrible and, by this time, covered both of my legs from my foot to above my knees. Both legs had turned a purplish color and my legs had begun to seep water. They were so painful that I could not bear to stand on them. Richard's parents consulted a witch doctor. He was familiar with dealing with evil spells. In his work, he employed a considerable amount of *yagona* (kava) which is the local drink mixed from pepper-root and used for ceremonies on every occasion, much like we use alcohol. Kava was mixed and poured in order to dispel the evil spirit.

About this time I felt I could stand it no more, and Richard knew it was time for him to take matters into his own hands. He put me into the car with as many clothes as I would need and drove me the 65 miles along the Queens Road to the capital, Suva. We stayed at his Aunt Caroline Dudley's home and Doctor Low was called in. She was a lovely Chinese doctor who still evokes kind memories with her smiling face and gentle ways. She laid her hand on my huge repulsive legs and just shook her head. She prescribed some tiny white tablets and told me that I would feel a lot better tomorrow and she would look in on me after her hospital rounds.

Aunt Caroline was the fraternal twin sister to Richard's mother. She was a large, robust woman with snow-white hair, as different from Ma's small frame, as was day from night, and yet they were devoted twins. She took me into her heart and mothered me as if I were her own. She waited on me hand and foot, even though she had house servants who could have done it for her. Her house was large and airy, surrounded by lovely flower gardens. Brass bowls and trays gleamed in every room and the bare floor glowed from frequent polishing.

Auntie Carrie's house was always full as she was a kind woman, and not a week went by that someone did not pop in from the countryside, or a distant city for an extended stay. Richard himself had stayed with her for several years in the past and considered Aunt Carrie his second mother. I improved rapidly in this environment. The pills took immediate effect, and the next day the swelling had begun to dissipate. Within a short time I was hobbling around, and in a week I was anxious to get back to Debbie and Ricky. Richard had stayed with me during the whole time.

Wallace had married Kini; a beautiful young woman whose father was Chinese and mother was Fijian. They had five children by the time we arrived in Fiji. Kini was a lovely, hard working person who always tried to help in every way she could to make my life and work easier. When I asked if I could use her sewing machine, she had two big Fijian men deliver it to my house. After a while, Kini decided she couldn't do without a refrigerator any longer and soon a lovely fridge was sitting in her house. However, since it was the only one in the compound, it soon went the way of my washing machine. Everyone began storing their meat and butter, eggs and milk there. I wondered if she ever had room for her own food. Kini and Wallace eventually had four more children making a total of nine. All through the years that I lived in Fiji, Kini was my most loyal and steadfast friend. She helped me through many ups and downs, sickness and health, births and weddings, and deaths. I could count on her always being there for me. We formed a bond that was as close as sisters. We remain so to this day.

With Wallace and Richard helping out in the mill, it was soon decided to expand the timber operation. Dad went into negotiations and obtained a concession of virgin timber covering five square miles. The forest was so dense and some of the trees so large that, at one tree, it took five men holding hands to reach around the trunk. The concession was located in the Nausori Highlands in the hills above Nadi. In order to shift the present operations, a road had to be constructed from the main road to the proposed hill at the sawmill site, a distance of seventeen miles. A new mill had to be planned and laid out, laborer's family quarters and single men's barracks were constructed, homes built for all the family members, and a store opened. The present mill and machinery was to be sold to Navutulevu Village. All the preparation and the work building and planning took less than three months. It seemed we were just settling into our new life at Nadriyalewa, but soon it would be time to move again.

Chapter Three

ENCOUNTER WITH THE UNKNOWN

Humming softly to myself, I lit the stove and set the kettle on it for tea. I had been working in my kitchen preparing lunch. Sun shafts beamed through the windows and spread across a kitten, which was stretched out full length on the window ledge to absorb the warmth of the sun. Half turning, I saw the figure of a tall Fijian man scoot swiftly around the side of my house towards Ma's kitchen. He knelt down as he entered the door, which was the custom, then assumed a cross-legged position on the floor and proceeded to rattle off in Fijian. After a moment he jumped up, darted out of the door and, to my surprise, Ma was hot on his heels.

My heart began to pound. There was something about their manner, the urgency in their movement that told me that there was something wrong. I looked around for the children, but there was not a soul in sight. I shut off the Primus, and then took off in the general direction in which I had seen Ma go. I caught a glimpse of her towards the end of the row of laborers' houses. She turned into at the last one. When I reached the house I bounded up the two wooden steps. There, I met a sight that I shall long remember. The room was perfectly quiet, not a sound met me. Every inch of the room was packed with Fijian people staring, as if in a trance, at a prone female figure on the floor. Debbie and Ricky were sitting in their midst, conspicuous as two fish out of water. Ma spotted me about this time, and whispered for me to sit down quickly.

The girl on the floor moaned softly, and it was then that I noticed the big Fijian *marama* (Fijian lady) who had begun cradling her in her arms. The girl was bare from waist up and her huge, firm breasts glistened with coconut oil. Her eyes were closed and perspiration beaded her forehead. A convulsion seized her and immediately, six husky Fijian men, who had deployed themselves around her, reached out and grabbed her at various places on her body to hold her down. It was as if they were holding onto a python because she twisted and turned, fighting and struggling. All the while, her eyes were closed and she was saying things that I could not understand. I nudged the girl next to me and asked her what in the world was happening. She spoke one word, t*evoros* before her eyes returned to the struggling girl. The men were sweating with the effort of holding the girl down, and the man on one end with his arms around her ankles was being whipped around, as if propelled by a tremendous force.

The girl's body finally relaxed, and the woman at her head began to massage her face and body with oil. In a few minutes the seizures started again. After about an hour of this, one of the men began to talk to the girl, supposedly addressing the devil in her. From what I was told later, he spoke to it this way. "Look at you; are you not ashamed to have all the bosses' wives sitting here watching you? What quarrel do you have with this girl? Why trouble her? Here you are in broad daylight, causing all this trouble. Have you no shame for the bosses' wives? You ought to be ashamed of yourself." Evidently this prospect did put it to shame for the girl relaxed after listening to his words. Her face screwed up and tears began to flow.

At the sight of the tears, the room began to relax with a steady murmur, "Sa taqi. Sa oti" (She is crying. It is finished.) A satisfied smile came over the faces of the people who had been trying to help her. The girl rolled over and, for the first time, opened her eyes. She sat up; looked around and seemed as amazed to see us there, as we were at the experience she had just afforded us.

Outside of the house, Richard's cousin, Emma Work, told me the details of the story. It seemed the girl was in love with one of our mill-hands, and had run away from her village to live with him. Someone in his family was displeased, because they had him in mind as a husband for someone else. When the girl became pregnant, this complicated matters. A member of his family decided to take things into their own hands. They placed a spell on her and today's convulsions were the result. Later in the evening, we heard that the girl had been three months pregnant but suffered a miscarriage an hour after the bout with whatever it was that assailed her. When she was well enough to travel, her young husband asked for a few days off work and took the young girl, along with an offering (sevusevu) of *Yagona*, and a gift of a *Tabua,* (whales' tooth, an article of special value to the Fijians and used as a tribal presentation on all special occasions), to his family to ask for their forgiveness. He asked them to accept this girl as his wife. I saw them often after that, living, it seemed, in quiet contentment.

Chapter Four

May 1960

ON THE MOVE

It's time to move, move! Good grief, we just got here. It's true we had only been at Nadriyalewa for four months, and now it was time to move camp. I started the packing and could not believe the amount of things that we had accumulated in such a short time. I paused and looked around the clearing. I will not be sorry to see the last of this place.

While we were waiting for the trucks to come back and move us, Richard and I decided to have a night out at one of the resort hotels. Korolevu Beach Resort Hotel situated on a beautiful lagoon about seven miles from the mill. It was a world famous resort that provided evening entertainment of dancing to a lively band. It also provided my first initiation into my husband's taste for drinking, flirting, and making out with someone else's mate. The Island girls do not draw the line between single and married men, often-times a wife might just as well be a door post next to which her handsome husband is standing, for all the notice they take of you, or for that matter, for all they care about what you might think of their actions.

After I had taken about all of the entertainment I cared to for that evening, I decided that it was time to go home. My husband however was enjoying himself immensely and did not want to leave. After waiting for him in the mill truck for half an hour, together with a group of Fijian boys who were sitting on the back of the truck bed waiting for a lift home, I sent one in to tell Richard that if he was not coming, I would leave without him. Never having driven a truck as large as that before I was not too sure what to do, but my temper and determination were rising by the minute. Several of the workingmen were also lounging on the back of the Bedford truck, known by the Fijians as the "Seven Tonner." I suppose that was because of the seven-ton load of timber that it carried. I switched on the ignition and could tell by the printed diagram on the gear lever how to shift the gears. I pushed in on the clutch and revved up the motor. I could hear the boys jump off of the back of the truck, hit the gravel road, and take off running. Richard opened the truck door and leaped in just as I let out the clutch and pressed on the gas.

The seven miles back home sped by the window at an alarming rate. The only time I really caught my breath was lining up that huge truck for one of those narrow bridges. I thought I would surely leave some parts of the Bedford truck hanging on those single lane bridges, but we made it through alright. I pulled up in front of our door, switched off the engine, and walked into the house. My husband followed. He had not uttered a word the whole trip back and we went to bed in silence. Since news travels fast in Fiji, for a long time after that, whenever I drove through the villages, I would be met with happy greetings of "Seven Tonner" with much waving and smiling.

The move began in earnest. We were to move to the Nausori highlands, just above Nadi. This was the hot dry side of the island. The side of the island where we had been living was the cool, wet side. So we left the cool green hills and shady palm trees and began to encounter dry hot, parched hills. We turned off of the Queen's Road just before reaching Nadi Town. The road took us high into the hills where we traveled a feeder road, constructed by the government, for two or three miles. From there, our tractors were working to make deep cuts, biting into the red clay of the hills, digging and forming the road that was to lead us 17 miles into the heart of the virgin timberland.

The first trip we made was by Land Rover, hazardous by anyone's description. When we reached the mill site, Dad was sitting in the shade in front of a one room building that later would be the company store. He was supervising half a dozen men who were laying out string lines to mark the foundation of the mill. He asked us where we would like to live. Richard looked around, pointed to a little knoll, where a solitary tree was struggling to survive the fierce heat. Dad looked up at the hill and nodded. It was as simple as that. When next I saw that hill, a cozy four-room house stood there, complete with electricity, ready for us to move in.

Somewhere I had heard the phrase, "It was the best of times, it was the worst of time," and so it was with my life in Fiji. The fierceness of the sun brought everything into sharp relief. The flowers were brighter, the sea was bluer, the sky was clearer than anything I had ever experienced.

During the four months we spent at Nadriyalewa, my husband and I would row out on the bay, throw the anchor over the side of the boat, and peer down to the sea bottom twenty to thirty feet below. The water was the color of a robin's egg, and brightly colored fish darted here and there. It was a world, which I, a farm girl from Ohio, who had never seen the ocean before crossing it, could never have imagined existed. I peered over the edge of the boat as if it were a doorway through which I, a stranger, was viewing some ancient and wonderful city.

In the years that I spent in Fiji, I never lost my awe of the sea. In the beginning, I used to sit on the shore under a palm tree so homesick, that often as not I gazed through tears wondering what was going on in that other world, the world that I had left so recently, and yet so long ago. The sea was calm and smooth as glass, but I knew the sea to be as fickle. Like a fiery tempered woman, it could be smooth and beautiful one minute, and stormy and evil the next. I gazed over the ocean asked, where does your wrath come from causing you to boil up, churn your insides, and make you toss boats around like they were toys, claiming lives of frightened souls? Little did I dream that one day I, and my whole family, would be in one of those boats at the mercy of the sea.

I lay back on the warm sand, gazed up at palm trees stretching seventy feet in the air. The leaves filtered back the sun and made patterns on the clusters of nuts way up in the tree. It is said that a coconut has three eyes with which to see where they fall, but, from my experience, if you are standing under a tree when that coconut is ready to fall, it is going to hit you, eyes or no eye. Believe me, from a height of seventy to one hundred feet, they hit the ground like bullets. Although I only heard of one person who was ever killed by a coconut dropping and hitting him on the head.

Chapter Five

June 1960

LONELY VIGIL

While we were waiting for our house to be completed at the new mill site above Nadi, we stayed in temporary housing. The doors had not been hung, so we had to prop them up in the frame at night. About this time Richard and his father had to go away to Australia to buy the new equipment for the mill, leaving us alone for two weeks.

On a gray, windy morning, a few large raindrops splashed in the dust outside of our structure. Before long the sky began to grow dark. The wind came up and I looked apprehensively at the doors propped up in their frames. Our furniture and belongings were piled in the corners and the mattresses were spread out on mats on the floor. The thunder flashed and the rain began. I lit the benzene light and began to prepare dinner. With a gust of wind the door blew flat to the floor and the rain and wind whipped through the house. The children and I struggled to replace the door and find something to prop it up. We mopped up and had a rather cold meal, then lay down on the damp mattresses to spend a miserable night alone listening to the rain beating against the tin roof.

The road to the new mill above Nadi was cut around mountains, down gullies, over creeks, and through flat land. In the hot sun the red clay dried hard and firm, but in rainy weather, it became dangerous and slippery. We never knew when we left for a day of shopping in Nadi Town whether we would make it home, or whether we would be spending the night on the road stuck in the mud. With Richard off to Sydney with his father and brothers, without a television, phone, newspaper or stereo and, now, without a husband, the children and I tried to find things to occupy our time.

The company houses were scattered on several hills. The laborers' barracks were down near the mill beside the company store. Our house was a little higher and we could look down on most of the activity. Looking up to the far-off hills, you could see in the distant darkness, the lights of the timber trucks returning from town, after delivering their loads. We would sit and watch them snake slowly down the hill, sometimes disappearing from sight in a dip in the road. Soon we would hear the heavy engines grinding closer to home. Sounds travel on the still night air, dogs barking, and children crying. We passed our time thus, waiting until the reason for us being there would return home, and our lives would start again. When Richard returned bringing with him the new machinery and an engineer from Australia to help with the installation, the work setting up the new sawmill began in earnest.

Things were stirring in the barrack. It seemed that one of the laborers' wives was missing and since she was almost ready to give birth; her husband had asked Dad if he would institute a search. Most of the able-bodied men joined in the search and went off in all directions looking for her. After several hours they returned, carrying the woman and her baby on a makeshift stretcher. It seems that the baby did not belong to her husband but to a secret lover and she had decided to kill the baby, but after giving birth out in the bush she found that she could not do it. Too weak to get home, she had to wait until someone found her. I saw her often after that, smiling and carefree. The child grew healthy and happy, seemingly unaware of his traumatic beginnings.

One evening I was feeling ill and decided to go to Ma for help. I cut through our yard, down the hill and over into Ma's compound. My eyes had become very red and irritated.

As soon as Ma saw me she said, "*Isa*, my child, what is wrong with you?" She immediately set too fixing my eyes. She rounded up Dad, stuck a lit cigarette in his mouth, and instructed him to blow the smoke into my eyes. He repeated this until she was satisfied and I was nauseous. It did not improve my eyes but Ma was satisfied she had done all she could.

On our way back home we cut through my yard and came upon three dogs stretched out in the heat, an unlikely place for Fijian dogs that usually seek the coolness under the house. I looked at Ma in question. "They're dead," she said. It seems the dogs licked the raw '*kaikoso*' that were picked from the reef in Nadi. It took a little while for me to digest the fact that the dogs had died from the remnants of my lunch that day. We had taken the raw flesh from the shellfish and eaten them with lemons and chilies, then discarded the shells. "But we ate them," I said in rising panic.

"I know," Ma said. "We can eat them, but dogs can't." I looked at the shells, then at the dogs and thought "Mother of Mercy!" Never again was *kaikoso* served at our house. I have no doubt that Richard ate it again, but not from my hands.

My eyes grew steadily worse. I think Ma was getting discouraged at this American daughter-in-law who did not respond to any of her Fijian remedies. Maybe it was because I did not believe in them. I was more used to pills and lotions, not leaves and barks of trees. But the longer I lived in Fiji, the more I grew to depend on the natural herbs and medicines of the old medicine women and men.

One of these old medicine women was Auntie Fanny Rounds, Ma's oldest sister. As long as I knew her she had cataracts in her eyes, but even then well into her nineties and half blind she could find her herbs and her tree bark. She would grind, boil and simmer them, or bind concoctions up in coconut fiber stripped from the coconut tree. It was fine and pliable as a roll of gauze. When Auntie Fanny doctored you, you were cured of whatever ailed you, upset stomach, headaches, boils, and infected mosquito bites. She had an herb for each one. Auntie Fanny was a kind gentle medicine woman. She was very nurturing. Anything we wanted to know about the island or about the family, we would ask Aunty Fanny. She had an answer to everything. She and her husband, Joseph Rounds, had fifteen children. She was the oldest in Ma's family of eight. A year after Ma had died we went back to Fiji for the summer, Aunty Fanny came out to spend the summer with us. It was her way of trying to fill the void that Ma's passing had left for us.

When we moved to the Nausori highlands, it was the first time that some of the villages of the interior had ever seen a Caterpillar tractor. There were many more wondrous things to follow that were strange sights to the interior village people. After the roads were completed to the sawmill, for the first time the villagers were able to load their produce onto a truck and take it down to market in Nadi. Before we arrived, the produce was packed on horseback and carried out. But, with the opening of the new road, life became easier for them. It was talked about in the village, that the American woman had a washing machine. Even though the washing machine had a gasoline engine, it did the job quite well. Often times, I would be doing my washing while a group of women from the nearby villages sat around cross-legged on the ground, watching me with much laughing and giggling. Sometimes they even brought their lunch to sit and marvel at how wonderful this machine was that washed and rung your clothes with such little effort on your part.

From Nadi, I ordered a kerosene refrigerator. In the outback, having such a luxury was unheard of. Unfortunately, when the fridge came, it didn't work. I filled the tank with kerosene and lit the wick and waited for it to get cold but nothing happened. Wallace said he would bring the repairman out on his next trip to Nadi, to come and have a look at it. After a couple of weeks the repairman came. After inspecting it thoroughly, he said there was nothing wrong with it that it just had to be turned upside down to circulate the Freon gas. I was dumbfounded at this suggestion, but since I did not know about these things the repairman assured me doing so would fix my problem. It seemed rather strange to me, but strange was beginning to be commonplace now.

After a week of the fridge standing up side down, the repairman came back again, fired up the fridge, and again nothing happened. It took another month before he admitted there must be something wrong with the refrigerator and agreed to take it back and send out a new one. The new fridge arrived with a big dent in the door, but at least it worked. It was not until later that we found out that the new replacement fridge had fallen off of Wallace's truck when he was bringing it in as he neglected to tie it down. We still fire up this same old fridge every summer when we go home to Fiji from the Bay Area. It has been faithful for over thirty-five years and the dent is still there.

On our trips into Nadi for shopping, I would meet Richard's school friends, and hear a great deal about how mischievous, and yet how smart, he was as a schoolboy. He had always been first in his class, but it seems like he was first in the mischief department, too. He liked nothing better than to antagonize two opponents and get them to fight each other, or to stand under the latticed porch and spy up the Sister's skirts as they walked past. The convent where he went to school was named Saint Joan of Arc. It was located in Sigatoka, about thirty miles along the coast from Naboutini Bay. Years later, when Richard and I went to France, we located the spot where St. Joan was jailed and later burned at the stake. Richard sent a postcard back from the site to the sisters in Sigatoka at St. Joan of Arc School. They were very happy to receive a postcard from such a hallowed place.

Richard, and the other children who boarded with him in St. Joan of Arc, were always hungry. His breakfast at the convent would consist of two slices of sourdough bread and a cup of weak tea, or sometimes lemon tea. For lunch, often it would be *kai* (shellfish), soup and *tavioka*, (cassava root) and for supper, again *kai* soup and *tavioka*. Occasionally, he would steal the Sisters' chickens, take them up in the bush, kill and pluck them, make a fire and barbecue them with a group of hungry children. At the time, Pa was driving a bus from Suva to Nadi and would stop by the school and drop food off at the convent for the children to eat. But it seems like very little food drifted down to the children. On weekends, the children would go to the homes of nearby relatives to get a good meal.

Dad's bus was the first bus in 1936 to run from Sigatoka to Korolevu when that section of road opened that year. The Fijian people made up a song about Dad that has been sung down through the years.

> *Tou Vodoka ga koya Raja na lori Savasava*
> *Sero Mai O Raja.*
> *Esirova Na wavu O tu Vavu.*
> *Lets ride that one and only,*
> *Raja has the cleanest Lori.*
> *Raja is coming down the hill.*
> *Over the bridge of Tuva...*

The fare from Korolevu to Sigatoka was two shillings. Dad also ran a store at Korolevu. During the years of WWII, the store catered to American soldiers who were stationed at Nadi and Suva. Dad was an enterprising businessman. He ran the store until 1947, when the Korolevu Beach Resort Hotel was built over the store site.

The power of a good education was the upper most prize to attain. Children were universally encouraged to endure any hardship in order to finish their schooling. One time, I met a lady in Nadi who showed me a three-inch scar on her wrist. She told me that she and Richard got into a fight when she was nine, and he cut her with a pocketknife. I was shocked, but they seemed to have a good time remembering those old times.

But one prank ended Richard's school years for good, landing him in an apprenticeship program in Suva. This happened when he and some school friends, Bobby and Lilly Smith, stole the railroad handcar and went for a joy ride, up and down the sugarcane railroad tracks. They returned it, with none the worse for wear. However, his father heard about his latest prank and locked Richard in the banana storage shed of their home in Korolevu where he spent two days without food, eating only bananas. His mother snuck him food when she could, but from Easter Saturday until Monday morning, he remained in the shed.

Ma's twin sister, Auntie Carrie came out to Korolevu for the Easter weekend to visit, and feeling pity for him, she asked if Richard could come home with her. Dad agreed to this. So Auntie Carrie and her husband, Uncle David Dudley, put Richard into a welding apprentice program at Bish Limited, where Uncle David was an accountant. Richard was fourteen years old at the time. This trauma seems to have never left him. Every year at Easter time, especially Good Friday, Richard gets sad and withdrawn. He stayed in the apprentice program for three years. Then started working on the cargo ships that sailed out of Australia to the Solomon and other islands. In 1947, one of the ships brought him to the United States West Coast, where he dreamed of returning. He continued working this way until 1950-51, when he got a chance to sail on the 'Lakeba' back to the United States. This time he stayed, and later met me.

Chapter Six

Unto, Nadir 1961

IN THE HIGHLANDS

It was in the highlands above Nadi that I became pregnant with our last baby, Diane. On a trip down to Nadi for my seventh month check-up, the skies became dark and the wind whipped up. We hurried through our shopping and headed out of town and back up the hill towards home. We had traveled ten miles when the heavens opened up and soaked the earth. We could look back down the hill and see Nadi in the distance still in bright sunshine. Our progress became slower and the road more slippery, until Richard finally stopped the car and decided it would be safer if we proceeded on foot.

We soon came to a deep cutting in the road and, to our dismay the muddy water was rolling through at an alarming clip. Richard was sure that he could make it, but not at all sure about me. But our choices were to either try to cross the creek, or spend the night back in the car. A Fijian man came along about then and Richard took advantage of the opportunity to ask him for assistance. With the extra hand supporting me, I waded out into the churning muddy brown water; the current whipped my legs and the rocks made our steps unsteady. By mid-stream the water was up to my chest and inching up towards my neck. I thought about my mother in Ohio, and wondered what she would think if she could see me now. We made it safely across and walked the rest of the way home looking like two wet hens, but none the worse for wear.

One evening, for want of something to do, I went down the hill at dusk to visit Ma. Most of the time you can just drop in on people, but tonight I found Ma had visitors. The local witch doctor was in to do a little pouring of the *yagona*. Now you must understand that Ma was a devout Catholic, but she was also true to her Fijian roots and sometimes she had to take matters into her own hands. In the candlelight, I saw a man dressed in the white loincloth of a Hindu priest. His face was painted with strange symbols, and he had skewers pierced through his cheeks and the skin on his chest.

My presence seemed to inspire him to greater intensity as he chanted, scattered marigold leaves about, then chanted some more. Since I could not understand his words, I soon grew bored and decided to leave. He admonished Ma not to let me go because if I did I would encounter a white dog, who was the devil. I was tired and I did not feel threatened so I left anyway. I said my goodnights and set off across the compound in the moonlight. As I crossed the road and started up the path towards my home, there, reflected in the moonlight near the bushes was a white dog. I stood and stared at the dog and the dog stared at me. I was wondering how the man knew that the dog would be in just this place. If it were a devil, it should probably be manifesting something devilish about now, but it appeared to me to be just an ordinary dog. I decided to continue along the path and never saw the white dog again.

Working away in my kitchen, I had applied a cleansing mask for my face, when it dries it turns white. I heard a knock at my open door I hesitated to turn around, knowing what I must look like. After a few seconds there was nothing to it but to see who it was. There stood a tall Fijian man, who had come to deliver a message. He tensed visibly, but to his credit he delivered the message, and then turned promptly and hurried off. I know that I was the talk of the barracks at suppertime.

I had moved up from a one-burner primus to a three-burner kerosene stove. It was not a very educated choice since anything that boiled over sent flames sputtering up around the pot. Eta, my Fijian 'house girl', refilled the new kerosene stove but in her haste neglected to screw the cap on tightly. Within minutes of lighting the burner, the stove erupted in flames. I grabbed a rug from the floor and attempted to smother the fire. It took some doing but soon the flames were out. I sat down on the floor and cried. Then I got mad. I picked the stove up and pitched it down the hill. It lay there for several days.

Everyone ignored it, too polite to comment on it, acting as if it were a common occurrence instead of a housewife gone mad. After a week, one of the laborer's wives inquired of Ma if she thought the *marama* (lady) would mind if she took the stove. Ma thought it was a good idea and I saw the lady happily carting it off to her house. I scoured the papers and found what I wanted in the want ads, a nice, prim and proper green propane stove on which I cooked for the next fourteen years.

One Sunday morning, we were on our way to church. The sun was warm and pleasant on our arms. The breeze flattened the long grass as it blew against the side of the hills. Not a cloud in the sky, a perfect day for our trip to Nadi. As we were traveling along the crest of the hill, we looked up and coming towards us on the one lane road was Richards' cousin, Sam Rounds, his wife Helen and their two children. The hill sloped sharply down on both sides of the road for several hundred feet. We knew there was no chance of passing each other safely so we stopped, but to our horror Sam's car kept coming. Little did we know at the time that his brakes had failed him.

We braced ourselves for impact but to our surprise and dismay, because he did not want to hit us Sam decided to drive around us. He passed to the right of us and just as the two cars were side by side, in the brief moment when the two families were looking at each other, Sam's car tilted on the narrow crest and started to slowly roll over. We heard the sound of metal crunching as the car rolled over and over down the hill. We were frozen in our seats, afraid to move for what we would see at the bottom of the hill. Luckily, the car came to a rest halfway down the hill. The front passenger door had come open and acted as a wedge to brace the car from further movement. Sam was half-in and half-out of the car.

The children were safe, but the baby, Thomas, was nowhere to be found. We looked all over but there was no sight of him. We listened, but there was no sound. The silence was ominous. We did not want to find what we were sure we would. Finally, to our surprise, we found Thomas lying snug and cozy in some bushes about twenty feet from the car. We looked at little Thomas and he looked at us. He had a bump on his head. Whether he was dazed from that bump, or just a plain good baby, I never figured out. He did not require any further medical attention and never seemed to be the worse for it. His mother, Helen, was not as fortunate. Her hand was badly mangled and, by the time we got her to hospital in Nadi she was nearly in shock. Helen recovered eventually but that day has never been erased from our memories.

Chapter Seven

Martintar, Nadi   January, 1961

CATHOLIC BOARDING SCHOOL

It was time for Debbie to go to school. I had not given much thought as to how she would do this because I just assumed that there was some school close by for her to attend. Richard soon made me aware of the fact that there was nothing close by and we would not be able to take her back and forth every day, so she would have to board at the St. Mary's convent school in Nadi. I can still recall the ache in my heart at the thought of this, as she was only five and a half years old. We had never been apart and I could not believe that my husband could ask me to send this small child off to live with strangers. After all, she was only a baby. I could see that he was as affected by this as I was and since I had no other alternative I reluctantly agreed to let her go.

The nuns tried to be as sympathetic as they could be to the crying children and distraught mothers, but Debbie's crying spell lasted longer than one old nun could endure and she said, "I guess we will have to move the school to Debbie, instead of bringing Debbie to the school." We just had to tear ourselves away and leave her crying there on the porch.

Richard and I did not handle the separation very well. Most times we would sit down to dinner and I would start crying at the empty place at the table.

One day a letter came for us from Debbie. It was brought back from Nadi by one of the truck drivers after delivering a load of timber in town. When I read Debbie's letter telling us how lonely she was, I began to cry and then Richard started crying, so we both sat there trying to eat and continued crying. The truck driver just looked at this sad sight shook his head and walked away.

Debbie was in school with her two cousins Joan and Louise. Five other children were boarding at the school with Debbie, the Guruwaiya children, four sisters Virginia, Norma, Rosa, Linda and one brother Basil. They were the children of our friend Paul Guruwaiya. Paul's wife, Gracie had recently died and since Paul worked on a ship as chief engineer, he had to put his children into boarding school too. Some weekends, all the children would come home with Debbie. Debbie was able to pick up a little Hindustani from them. One evening, after I had tucked them into bed they continued chatting away. So I whispered to Richard to tell me, how to tell the children to quiet down and go to sleep, in Hindi. There was complete silence for a minute, until one of the girls turned to Debbie and said, "How did she do that? She doesn't know how to speak Hindi?"

One day, at the convent, Debbie decided she needed to get away and went to visit some friends of ours who lived a short distance from the school. Unfortunately, she neglected to ask permission of the nuns. When our friends realized the situation she was returned to the school the next day. The Sisters decided that the only fitting punishment would be to whip her legs with an inch thick rubber strap until it left angry welts up and down her small legs. She was to miss her supper and spend the night standing upright in the dining hall. So there she stood, alone, hungry and scared in that big dark room.

Her cousin, Louise, saved a *roti* (flat bread) smeared with golden syrup from her dinner. When she thought the nuns had gone to sleep, she crept out into the dining hall and stayed with Debbie until one of the Fijian teachers came out and sheltered Debbie in her room until the first light. I have seen some of Debbie's friends wearing t-shirts saying, "I survived Catholic boarding school." Eventually the separation got to be too much for us and we rented a house in Tamavua, just above the city of Suva, where it would be possible for the children to go to school and still have a home life. However, this meant that Richard and I would be separated, and only see each other on weekends. Even later school created a problem for us, trying to keep the children with us and also trying to get them educated. Years later I joined with some of the parents to start a building fund through bake sales, bazaars and begging to build a school at Korolevu on land connected to the Saint Peter Channel church. Father Shiu and Mrs. Cathy Clark spearheaded the venture. We petitioned the bus company to put on a special bus to pick the children in time for school. To our consternation we found the when the school was ready it would only accommodate one class, adding another class each year. Diane grew with the school, but there was still Debbie and Ricky. Mrs. Clark, the daughter of Sir Hugh Ragg, who owned the Korolevu Hotel, and a string of other hotels around the Island, and her husband Bill had decided to home school their children Stephanie, James and Chris. They invited my children to join them there at Korolevu. Margret an Australian teacher was hired, and Ricky and Debbie started school. How wonderful to see them off every morning and home every evening.

From Korolevu Rick and Debbie transferred to Saint Joan of Arc in Singatoka their father's old school. Debbie persevered but Ricky found that the one and a half hour bus ride each way, arriving at school dusty tired and motion sick became too much for him. We decided to place him in the Marist Brothers School at Vatuwaqa where some of our top leaders in Fiji had attended. Boys will adapt. One day I over heard him talking about how good the roti and curry was and asked him, "if the school made roti for all those children?" The conversation went something like this: "No that was when I ate with the gardener. So why did you eat with the gardener? He said, because all the paw paws were green and I couldn't find anything else to eat. So why are you hunting for paw paws, to eat? Because I was hungry!" he stately matter-of-factly. There we had it, the same problem that caused his father to steal the Sisters chickens and take them up in the bush and roast them over a campfire. Ricky later transferred to Vuniniu Indian school where he learned Hindi, and then to Korovisilou Fijian school, where he learned Fijian. One thing he also learned was how to adapt to any situation.

Chapter Eight

Tamavua, Suva 1964

HONEY

We continued to live in our rented house in Tamavua, while we waited for our new house to be finished at Qaviu on Naboutini Bay. One day the baby nurse, Mereoni, who had been hired to help me with Diane, arrived at work with a small black and white ball of fur. We promptly named her Honey, and she and Diane became inseparable. Now Honey was a different matter altogether because she did not realize she was a dog. She thought she was a member of the family. From the time she came to live with us, she knew that we were her family and she loved each one of us equally. On our trips to Naboutini for the weekend, Honey was always the first one in the car. We often called her Diane's shadow, as it seemed that Honey followed her every footstep, but it was in the back yard where her talents really showed.

Honey knew that the back yard was her private domain and she did not suffer fools lightly. It happened that our back yard was the shortest point between two villages and the Fijian people used to climb over our fence and cut across our yard to use this short cut. Honey decided she was having none of this. She lay on the back porch, head resting on her paws, seemingly asleep, eyes half closed. Her innocent victims would climb the fence, glance at the sleeping dog, and attempt to proceed on their way. Honey would wait patiently until her victims were right in the middle of the yard. Then, she would then hurl herself at the trespassers with many a snarl and a yelp. The startled young men would leap for the fence, launching themselves up and over. Honey always allowed her opponents enough time to make it over the fence without drawing blood. She felt her fierceness was enough to get the job done. After a time, our backyard was soon cleared of unauthorized traffic.

The house rule was that no dogs were allowed in the bed, but that law did not apply to Honey. Invariably when I would tuck the kids in bed, one or the other of them would have a suspicious lump in the bed. With angelic looks on their faces, they would deny any knowledge of Honey's whereabouts. Knowing that she would have to sleep outside if she were discovered, Honey would remain as quiet as a mouse. I would pretend not to notice the telltale ripple of the blanket at the mention of her name.

Honey's job was not only to guard the back yard and follow in Diane's footsteps, but it was also her mission in life not to let the hated mailman deliver the mail. Every afternoon at two p.m. we had to shut her in the house, or miss our mail delivery. I never knew how dogs could tell time, but right on time she would post herself at the end of the side walk and wait for the school bus that would bring Ricky and Debbie home from school. Rain or shine, Honey stuck to her post until she saw Ricky and Debbie safely into the house and so she dispensed with another one of her duties.

One day, when Diane and I returned home from shopping, the house was quiet. No excited barking, no Honey to greet us. As the evening progressed, we became more and more alarmed. The children searched the neighborhood, but she was nowhere to be found. Richard came in late from the mill and was met by gloom all around. Dad must do something to find her. The only possible explanation was that the Humane Society truck had picked her up. Even though it was way past closing time, Richard went off to the pound since we were unable to bear the thought of Honey spending the night in a cage by herself.

A short while later, the car returned and we could hear the excited barking. Before we could get to the door, Honey launched herself into our arms with fervor heretofore unmatched. She raced in and out of each room of the house, barking joyously as she went, greeting each one in turn with a slurping face lick. I really do not know who was happier, the dog or us.

Our life with Honey was a short three years. She met her demise under the wheel of a car, plunging us into sadness at the loss of one who had filled our life with so much love. We wrapped her little body in a fine, hand-woven mat and tied it with ribbons. We all piled into the car for the trip to Naboutini and dug a grave under the mango tree by the powerhouse, and laid Honey to rest. She would love it here under a big shade tree, with a clear view of the whole back yard, and the blue ocean beyond.

Dorothy and Claudius in the front yard at Qaviu

Qaviu 2000

Qaviu with the pool added in 1967

Qaviu 1964

The family at home in Qaviu 1971

The Debbie-Diane anchored on Naboutini Bay

Rebecca, Kajah, and Bumpa with our good friend and neighbor
Jone Lowanare

Fishing for King Mackerel with Bumpa and grandchildren

Rajah and Esther Ram
Pa and Ma, ages 29 and 30, photo taken in Lautoka 1938

Lella, Claude's sister, on her wedding day in 1958

"Momo" Atunaisa Ralia was a cannibal in his early youth
He died at the age of 106

Mereoni with Diane the day we got Honey
(Brown and white dog)

Mrs. Ulamila Gopal, our neighbor in Lami

Kini, (middle) visiting Aunt Marvene and Aunt Doris in Ohio after they visited her in Fiji
Picture taken in front of Eden Baptist Church

My mother, Evelyn Williams in California 1980

My father, Harold Williams on his wedding day, 1930

Rebecca, Nathan, Kajah, Shaun, and Chris. Pacifica, California, 1987

Family gathering in Pacifica, California 1996

Ricky, Cheryl, Shaun and Nathan. Christmas 1997.

50th Wedding Anniversary: Deborah, Dorothy, Claudius, Diane, and Richard

Dorothy 2004

Claudius 2004

Chapter Nine

Qaviu 1965

THE GREEN *BU*

The Queen's road snakes around the point like a giant black serpent with a white stripe down his back. Equally as deadly as the curves in the road, are the blind corners, whose danger is often combined with speed and sometimes alcohol. The road has claimed the lives of sixty people so far this year. The house, which we finished, building in 1964, sits high on a hill overlooking the Pacific Ocean. It looks lovely and inviting. Its white paint is brilliant in the tropical sun. The windows are trimmed in bright aqua. A long verandah runs twenty-eight feet along the front.

While sitting in the yard, under the lemon tree, my observations are interrupted by three young brothers and a sister, who are searching for more *bu* (green coconut) for their coconut drink stand down by the road. It never ceases to amaze me that the Fijians do not bother to plant coconut trees themselves. Our planted trees have provided the local villagers with hundreds of coconuts over the years. Even our lemon trees are fair game, as they think nothing of walking a half a mile to our back yard, producing a long pole, and proceeding to knock down whatever lemons they may need for their dinner. Even though they have to walk that far, it does not occur to them to plant a tree right in their own back yard.

Today my scavengers have gathered a bag of ten or twelve bu. I ask the girl, Ruci what they did with the money. She gave me a serious look and said that they buy sugar, tea and bread. No frivolous chocolate and comic books for this gang. Nimi, the oldest of the group, listened to our conversation while he stripped the bark from a pole he was carrying. When he was finished, he tied it into a long loop, took it to the nearest tree, slipped his feet into it and hiked himself smoothly up the tree. Soon the ground was pelted with fresh *bu*. "Hold everything", I said, "While I get my camera." He obliged me and soon was smiling and waving from the top of the tree some fifty feet above ground.

When I had finished filming, I rewound the tape and let them see themselves and only wished I had another camera to record their expressions. With much giggling and whooping they passed the camera and ear phones around between them. Fourteen *bu* later, they hoisted their bags and disappeared down the path through the underbrush, their brown feet crushing the wild fern growing there. I noticed that Ruci, the only girl, had the biggest load of all. So much for equal rights here.

When day turns into evening the sun slides down behind the mountains to our right over the abandoned rice fields, silhouetting the coconut branches in a red hue. I can see a Fijian couple going home along the road from the plantation. The man sits easily atop his horse leisurely riding along, while his wife walks behind nearly bent double carrying a load of firewood.

An evening star comes out, and it is so bright it seems as if it is a distant planet with all of its lights turned on. Never have I seen a star such as this. As the darkness begins to settle over the island, a full moon with a warm glow illuminates everything, a great time for walking the beach, or strolling the yard, or watching from the veranda the ripples on the water sparkling like diamonds along a silvery path.

On dark nights, no streetlights illuminate this small corner of the world. But far off in the distance, some eighteen miles across the ocean, the intermittent flash of the lighthouse on Vatulele can be seen. Sometimes, a glowing cruise liner passes by like a fairy ship in the night. With binoculars, you can see people strolling the decks and if you are very quiet, the faint sound of music can be heard across the water.

The darkness also brings out the wild cats from their hiding places in the bush to forage for food. I am always happy to see the yellow cat, as it reminds me of the old yellow cat that was Ma's cat, and our constant weekend guest. We lived in Tamavua, Suva, during the week a distance of some fifty miles away, but always came back to Qaviu for our weekends. Ten minutes after our arrival, you could set your clock on this because the old yellow cat was punctual, he would come trudging up the first turn of our hill, on into the straight, and around the second turn past the mango tree.

Age never seemed to slack his speed, just one steady paw in front of the other one. Our dogs never bothered him as he made his way down the sidewalk into the back door, through the kitchen and into the living room. There he stayed, never to leave until Sunday rolled around, where from the car's rear window, we could see him retrace his steps down the hill to spend the week with Ma until we returned the next Friday. On our final trip down the hill, when we were returning to the States, the old yellow cat trudged unconcerned behind our car never suspecting that it would be the last time he would see his weekend guests. On our summer returns to Fiji, we always left food out on a saucer in the night hoping that some of the old yellow cat's son's or daughter's would benefit from his long ago friendship with us. They did but never tarried long over their food, flitting back to the safety of the bush and darkness.

The smell of the *beka* (flying foxes) would reach me on the night air. I would look up at the sky full of those dark shapes swirling to feed on the fruit trees at night and returning at first light to hang upside down in their caves to sleep away the unwelcome daylight. Frogs would jump and croak and occasionally miscalculate the distance and hop right into the swimming pool where they would paddle around until they would be retrieved and thrown out the next day with an "ugh!" by the kids. They say other creatures walk in the night here, however, never having seen any, I cannot comment on them. But the saying goes that if you meet a stranger in the night, and you wonder to which world he belongs, look at his feet. It is said here that spirit folk walk just above the earth, without their feet touching the ground.

I often sat on the front porch with my feet propped up on the railing. I remember our old dog Bruno hated those veranda bars. I can see him now in my minds eye, looking at me through these bars. I think Bruno, an old beat-up, pit bull rescued from the dog pound had at one time been imprisoned behind bars. He was battle-scarred and worn, a true warrior and a great watchdog, but bars were another thing. Some experience left a bad taste in his mouth. He would be as normal as any other dog, but just let him walk behind the iron railing on the front verandah, and he would take on a whole new personality. He would bare his teeth, and let out vicious growls and snarls, snapping his teeth and barking. This behavior was quite startling to us until we saw the pattern of it. Then we relaxed. On a slow day, we entertained ourselves and guests watching Bruno perform. Once you walked around the railing and came into full view, Bruno would close his mouth, bound over to you, and lick your hand and wag his tail, reminding you that you were his great and good friend regardless of what had just transpired. As long as he lived he never got over his anger at the iron bars.

Chapter Ten

1970

THE RED PRAWN OF VATULELE

The big white bow of the thirty-nine foot cabin cruiser, the "Debbie-Diane", cut a smooth swath through the deep blue water. We were on weekend cruise to Vatulele Island from our sheltering at Naboutini Bay. We were loaded down with family and food. The island of Vatulele lay some eighteen miles straight south from our house. From our front verandah, we could see the outline of the island and, at night, the flickering of the lighthouse. Some twenty-eight of us, the entire family, all except Ma, Pa and little Kini were on board the sleek cruiser which was powered by twin Perkins Marine engines. We had a top cruising speed of eighteen knots. The cruiser was three years in the making, with timber milled from our own sawmill. It was our pride and joy.

The cruise to the island was smooth and fast, taking us an hour. We anchored in the clear water offshore and ferried ashore by small canoes. Vatulele is famous for their red prawns, which are considered sacred by the Fijians of the island. Alive and swimming in the clear pools, they are bright red, similar to the color of cooked prawns. Our young guide encouraged the children to swim in the fresh water pools containing the prawns though normally this is taboo. After a weekend of swimming, fishing, and lounging on the beaches we clamored back aboard for the return trip to Naboutini. One of the Fijian boys hitching a ride with us climbed top side and stood as lookout holding onto the mast atop the roof of the Debbie-Diane.

We traveled about a quarter of a mile past the reef, when all of a sudden we encountered stretch of rough murky water. Where just before the sea had been glossy and smooth. It was now choppy and small white caps appeared on the waves. In what seemed like a heartbeat, we were embroiled in heavy seas. Wallace, Richard's oldest brother, was at the wheel and saw that it was impossible for us to turn around and head back to Vatulele. He said that the only thing to do was to stay in the troughs between the swells. Everyone was beginning to get uneasy, and emotions turned into sheer panic as the seas became mountainous with waves that swelled to thirty feet and crashed down and over us. The three brothers began gathering their children around them as it looked as if this was one situation that we were not going to survive.

A trough would form and Wallace would head into and up it, bow first. We could look up and see the waves cresting far above our heads. Once over the wave, we would ride it down much like a surfer would. Thinking each time that the boat would turn over; we braced ourselves to ride the next wave. I have seen angry seas before, but never from this viewpoint. Wallace could do nothing but fight the wheel and steer the trough while we all hung on for our dear lives and prayed.

We were very fortunate that day. Six hours later we managed to limp our way out of the storm. As we neared the bay, we could see cars lining the road, and realized that Pa and Ma and the rest of the family had been keeping vigil, searching the waters for any sign of us, as we were so long overdue. We had reached the shore some seven miles below our starting point, and hugged the coastline back to our anchorage in the bay below our house. The Fijian boy was still clinging to the top of the boat when we anchored. Several years later, when we were recounting this tale, our daughter-in-law Cheryl, told us that she too had been onboard. She was one of the several small children that had accompanied us that day. I did not know then that she would grow up and marry our son. If you ask any member of the family, "What was your worst experience?" Everyone invariably says, "Our boat trip to Vatulele to see the Red Prawns."

Chapter Eleven

1971

WOMEN I ADMIRE

Mrs. Gopal was our neighbor when we lived in Lami, Suva. She is one of the women that I admire greatly. Not many women are put in that classification. Some I tolerate some I do not. Mrs. Gopal, I admired greatly. I have known her for nearly thirty years, ever since we moved in next door to her in the little community of Lami. She was petite and always had a child or baby near her. Her house looked down on mine. It nestled on a hill against the trees. She made me feel that whatever I said or did was all right with her. She never judged me, and she never called me by my given name. To her I was always "Diane's mother" but she did not choose to ignore Debbie or Ricky. Till this day, they are her children too, but to her I was especially "Diane's mother."

Her cooking is what attracted me to her at first. Despite all the children she had to cook for, there was always a plate or bowl of something special for us. One of her children, Kari, Joe, or John would show up at my back door with a covered dish, and no matter what I had cooked, hers was eaten first. She was never a bother and never intruded. If she was there, it was right for her to be there. When she was not there, I missed her. If I had a problem, she let me talk. She never judged, advised, or directed. She just listened and said, "Don't worry about it, Diane's mother, everything will work out." When it was apparent that things were not going to work out by themselves, she would mention that maybe we should just pray, I had no doubt that she included my problems in her prayers along with her many others. She must have made an impression on my children, too. Many years later when her husband, Mr. Gopal, lay very sick in bed, having lost a leg to diabetes, and facing the loss of his other, it happened that my son, Ricky arrived from the States to visit him. Within the hour, his son, John was there from Australia, and Joe, from the New Hebrides. They all arrived from such diverse places on the same day on their own, without prior planning. Mr. Gopal was deeply touched. He said, "My boys have all come home." It was not long before he went home to heaven, and I was happy that Ricky had been there to see him off before he departed.

~~~

I had visitors from the States, my father's sisters; Aunt Pauline and Aunt Marvene arrived from Ohio. Mrs. Gopal loved them, as she loved us, without reservation, complete and overflowing. The path from my back door up the hill to her front door was well worn now. No one went around by way of the sidewalk, which would take too much time. The business between her house and mine was urgent and important so we would just go straight up through the path. When my two Aunts were ready to go home to Ohio, she stood at the back door with a farewell gift and sang "*Isa Lei*" (the Fijian song of farewell) tears brimming over her eyes, and spilling from ours. It was touching and loving. I have heard it sung many times since, but I will never forget the time and place I heard Mrs. Gopal first sing this song.

~~~~

Ma was another woman that I admired. Sometimes we disagreed, and I am sure that I tried her patience many a time. Sometimes she tried mine, but I always admired her. Her life could not have been easy. Sometimes she looked so tired and worn. Sometimes she told me, "Dorothy, when I go to bed my nerves go like this," making a trembling motion with her hands. That is when she would get up, and sit in the dark smoking a cigarette. Sometimes Dad would wake up with her, and they would both sit up and smoke, inside their mosquito net. She would have to wash her net more often than most because of it.

They also enjoyed fruit such as apples and mangoes, when they managed to hide a few from their many grandchildren. Apples were a delicacy and imported from New Zealand. When Ma went to town, she would bring all the children apples, like we bring our children candy. But a few she would tuck under the bed for her and Dad to enjoy late at night when they could not sleep.

Ma accompanied Dad to India but I cannot remember what year it was, maybe around 1966. I am not sure she even wanted to go but she went. We have a picture of them standing in front of the Taj Mahal, the same spot where Richard and I stood some twenty-seven years later when we went to attend the wedding of our niece, Noleen, a spectacular affair, right out of the pages of Arabian Nights, but that is another story. The same spot where Debbie stood some twelve years after us on her way to Banaris to visit the birthplace of her Great-Grandfather Harbans.

They took the train across India and were caught in a fight between the Pakistanis and the Hindus. Riots were something so alien to Ma and Pa, and so traumatizing that Ma never really got over it. She said that she kissed the ground when she got off the plane back in Fiji. Whether she did literally or not, I am not sure; I do know that she kissed all of us, every last one of us. She said she thought she would never see us again. She brought us back beautiful sari's, rings made of silver filigree, peacock feathers, one-hundred-year bronze calendars, and stories of what she had seen, felt and done on her trip to India.

I loved Ma's sense of humor. She was always up for a good laugh. It was her business to entertain my two Aunts from Ohio. She cooked us a lovely dinner one evening and while we were relaxing on the couch afterwards, she excused herself saying she had something to show us. When she came back, this mild mannered little woman had transformed herself. Her hair was flowing freely down her back and she was stripped to the waist. She carried a large fan in one hand made of palm fronds, and a long wicked-looking spear in the other. Without further ado, she proceeded to sing, shout and leap about in a Fijian war dance. Our Ohio ladies sat transfixed, their mouths frozen open, eyes wide in astonishment. After the shock wore off, they let out whoops of laughter, clapping their hands with glee, spurring Ma on to greater efforts. Some of the best floorshows in some of the best hotels could not hold a candle to Ma's performance that night. The memory comes back to warm me on long nights, bringing a smile to my lips in the dark, and transporting me back in time to Ma's living room.

Chapter Twelve

Nov. 28, 1989

VERE'S MOTHER

On this day, Jane, my sister-in-law, and I had planned to go to Sigatoka to do some shopping, and to pick up her eye medicine. We met Francis, Wallace and Kini's oldest son, aged 19. He was on his way to Nadi. He told us that Vere's mother had died. Vere had worked for Kini in Suva, helping her with the children when they were small. Lella and I had just spent some time with Vere's mother on the previous Wednesday. In our conversation she had told us, to give her love to her daughter in the United States. I told her that Vere would be home soon. She was working on her papers to become a legal resident of the United States. Then, she would be able to travel freely back and forth to Fiji. Vere's mother said that it would not be soon enough. When Vere came home, she would find her over there, pointing with her finger. I asked Lella where she was pointing, and Lella told me she was pointing in the direction of the cemetery. I was shocked at how quickly Vere's mother's prediction came true. She died the following week.

On the day of the funeral, Jane, and her son, and I bought *yagona* or *kava*, a traditional offering for weddings and funerals alike. We took it along with an offering of money to the house where the *sevu sevu* (presentation of gifts) were being made. Our offering was given along with a speech by our spokesperson that was the *Mata ni Vanua* (Eye of the land.) The offering was accepted by one of the village elders.

A serving of *yagona* is made by having the root pounded into a fine powder then wrapped in fine matting from a coconut tree, which acts as a sieve. It is then mixed in a large wooden bowl with water. After this process of mixing, the drink is poured into a hollowed-out shell of half a coconut. The server, always a Fijian man, sometimes dressed in traditional dress, according to the importance of the ceremony, will grasp the cup on both sides between thumb and forefinger, and approach stiffly to the most honored guest first. Tradition requires one to drain the cup without any show of distaste on your face. When the cup is drained, you clap hands three times, while your audience chants *Maca!* (Empty.)

After the kava ceremony, Jane and I made our way to the Catholic Church where the mass was already in progress.

Vere's Mom lay in a wooden coffin at the foot of the altar. The coffin was covered with tapa cloth (material made from the bark of a tree and decorated with dye from crushed berries) and a trim of lace around the edge of the coffin lid. The Catholic priest read the prayers in Fijian, sprinkling Holy Water from a jar with a small green flower sprig. When the prayers were finished, six tall, young men stood up on either side of the coffin. They were all dressed in white shirts and dark *sulus* (Fijian style wrap-around cloth skirts.) They picked up the coffin and followed the priest out of the church.

Two altar boys dressed in white robes covered with red tunics carried the Cross and led the procession through the village. It was a solemn walk with the sounds of the choir still singing in the church. The path led through the village and out through the back to a pathway that would take us up a steep hill to the cemetery. Ahead of me, I could see the strong young men of Naimelimeli Village lifting the coffin up the side of the hill. When it came my turn to climb the hill I had to have a helping hand from Iliseva, an old friend who used to work for Ma years ago. She put her hand on my backside and pushed me up the steep slope. When we finally reached the crest of the hill, we were overlooking the village from under the spreading leaves of the *baka* trees. It was a fitting-resting place for a tired mother.

Prayers were said again, and the coffin nesting on huge mats was lowered into the grave. A young man jumped in and folded the mats over and around the coffin. Then, the moist red clay was shoveled onto the grave. We each threw in a handful of earth, wishing her speed on her journey to God. I was thinking how sad it was that a mother waited so long to see the face of her daughter, and that a daughter in America would never again see her mother. After the dirt was packed in and mounded over, the ladies who had been waiting patiently in the shade came forward and handed the men a long lovely piece of *tapa* that was placed like a blanket over the grave. Four decorative shrubs were cut and anchored at the four corners of the *tapa*. Other women came forward and laid the flower wreaths on top of the *tapa*. After a while we made ready to leave. I looked back over my shoulder and gazed at the quiet scene of the beautiful resting place.

The procession returned to the village where we sat outside the house that Vere had built for her mother. We had another bowl of *yagona* while watching the preparations for the feast that would follow. The *taro* and *tavioca,* (root crops) were put in the *lovo* (ground oven.) Beef was cut up and shared among the visitors, and some cooked for the people that would stay for the meal. Jane and I said our final goodbyes and were preceded from the village by a man bearing two rolled mats, one for each of us. A final handshake all around and we turned the car around and headed home.

When I returned home to the States, I sat with Vere telling her as best I could about her mother's funeral and her mother's last words. When Vere was finally able to return home to Fiji, she made that steep climb to the top of the hill to kneel beside the long ago *tapa* covered grave of her mother.

Chapter Thirteen

June 28, 1994

THE FIVE GRANDS

As our plane comes in over Nadi, I think of how little Fiji has changed in the forty years that we have been in and out of here. We see the same buildings and the same roads. It even seems like we see the same paint on the same houses. The only difference is that the faces have changed. Now we have come home with five new faces. Our five grandchildren accompany us over the summer season to this land of sea and sun, back to the house on the hill over looking the ocean. We come in and sweep away nine months worth of cobwebs, take off the dust covers, light up the old kerosene fridge, air out the pillows, and make everything fresh and clean again. Then, we have pandemonium for the two months of summer vacation.

It is hard work. Even with two house-girls to help me, it is not easy. There are huge meals to be cooked, water to be boiled for drinking. We used to heat bath water too, until the shiny new water heater came to replace the twenty-year-old one. There are wet towels, tons of wet clothes, mosquito bites, cut knees, sometime even doctor visits. When the day is bright and sunny, we spend it playing in the surf. Even on wet and drizzly days, there are new things to discover about these grandchildren of ours. Two of our grandchildren, Rebecca and Kajah, played in the shallow surf. Another one, Chris dammed up the fresh water stream. Shaun and Nathan, set out to make a shack to keep out the light rain. They made a very respectable four-post hut, lashed together with coconut leaf strands, roofed over with coconut leaves. Then, Shaun managed to build a fire even though the wood was mostly wet. So there we all sat on the beach, in our little hut with our feet toward the warm fire. I was happy and still a little sad, thinking of when I used to sit with my own children like this. Now, it is the grandchildren who are able to warm me with their campfire, yet they too are growing up so fast.

When we built our house in 1964, we built on top of a high hill with a panoramic view of the ocean. The house is open and airy and with tiled floors, sunken bath, and swimming pool a few steps from the front porch. The hill that we chose to build on, we later found out, was a favorite meeting place for ancient Fijian chiefs.

There are many legends in Fiji. One local legend has it that Fijian Chiefs of Navutulevu Village, upon their death, their souls used to follow the top of our ridge down to the point and jump. The face of the cliff has a sheer drop of some three hundred feet to the beautiful ocean below. The Fijian term for this legend is Rika rika ni yalo (a jumping place for the soul). When we built the house we made sure not to put any permanent structures in this pathway as advised by Jone Butolu our neighbor and dear friend, just in case the ancients were still using it. I feel it is very important to respect the old ways and traditions, even if sometimes we cannot understand them.

One night soon after we had returned to Fiji, I was asleep when I heard a knock at the back door. I got up and went to answer it. When I turned the corner from the hallway, I could see standing in the doorway, illuminated with light was a middle-aged Fijian man. He had on a black *Sulu* and white short sleeve shirt. He did not speak, but he gave me a radiant smile of welcome. That dream is still fresh in my mind. Strange things like this often happen in Fiji; things that make you wonder but also seem as normal as day and night.

~~~~

In the early years, Richard's cousin by the name of Louisa, used to wait near Komave Village for a ride with us to attend mass at the St. Peter Chanel church in Korolevu. Every Sunday we picked up Louisa and her husband Suli, who would wait by the side of the road near their home. Louisa was as short and plump, as Suli was tall and thin, but they were always together. One Sunday, after we had been away in the capital city of Suva for a couple of weeks, we found only Suli waiting on the road. He told us that Louisa had passed away the week before. Since we had not heard the news in Suva, we were not able to attend the funeral. So we went to Suli's house that Sunday evening and presented our *sevusevu* (offering) to Louisa's family. Suli did not live much longer after that. He seemed to visibly age after Louisa left. Then Seva, Louisa and Suli's son, started riding to church with us on Sunday. He was around our age and Richard had gone to school with him.

One Sunday in June, after we returned to Fiji for another summer, a lone young man stood on the road waiting for a ride. On the way to church, we discovered that this was Joseph, Seva's son. He said that Seva had died the month before. We told Joseph of all the years we had ridden to church with, first his grandparents, then his father and mother, and now with him. It was as if Seva had wanted his son to tell us good-bye.

Chapter Fourteen

August 1994

QAVIU

I am sitting in a swivel chair, my feet propped up, on another glorious day as only you find here in these surroundings. As a diamond would only be beautiful in a lovely setting, so too this day may not be the same twenty or thirty miles further on. Naboutini Bay cuts through the reef and runs diagonally into the horseshoe of land that is curved around it. Man Friday Beach Resort is on one point to our left looking southeast, and the bay curves gracefully around to our point, forming a sheltered cove. Yachts sail into it, running away from storms and wind, or running to a tranquil anchorage for a day, a week or a month. Hundreds of coconut trees sway in the wind, the oldest and tallest planted by us some forty years ago.

I remember how smooth and barren this hill was when we first climbed up here from the Fijian *bure* (thatched house) below. The big Fijian *bure* was the first structure to be built on this property. It was later torn down and a modern two-story home was built for Ma and Pa nestled in the circle of the two hills, on flat ground and close to the main road. None of that hilltop stuff for them, besides, what about hurricanes? A house sitting high atop a hill with a gull-wing roof spread out to the sky, "Why that will take off like a kite in a high wind come the first good hurricane," said Pa, when describing our house. Well, it has stood sound for forty years. Like a great lady, a little battered and bent from a hurricane or two, but still standing proud and beautiful.

The drive-way is lined by more giant coconut trees marching like silent sentinels along the road to a curve at the first turn, and continuing on up the steep slope until they march right to the top of the hill and join a giant mango tree standing guard at the top of the yard. Upon attaining the crest of the hill, most people stand in awe. Not at the low slung white house with the sloping roof, but at the deep blue ocean spread out 180 degrees around the foot of the hill some 300 feet below. The channel for the Naboutini Bay breaks the white line of the reef to our left, and the channel for Navutulevu Bay to our right.

The green lawn slopes down toward the cliff to give an uninterrupted view of the ocean and the eyes gaze off of the end of the swimming pool deceived into thinking that the pool and the sea are connected. The lawn is edged by more coconut trees, our neighbor planted his trees in a straight line down the hill from each of our trees, and they march away like soldiers until the top of the last tree can barely be seen over the edge of the lawn.

I see the fields where my best friend Viti Whippy and I would pick wild guavas, bring them home, and make luscious wild guava jam. Viti continues the practice, refining and perfecting, and now sells her jam which undoubtedly is one of the best jams you will find anywhere. My friends request jars of Viti's guava jam whenever they know I'm planning a trip home.

The reef is boiling with the force of water hitting it. It spills over the crest into Naboutini Bay joined by a tranquil expanse of blue-green water and white sand stretching out from the Man Friday Beach Resort. The water is darker on our side of the channel reflecting the seaweed and rocks beneath. Looking across the bay, I can see a Fijian *bure* clinging high atop a hill. Sometimes at night from my bedroom, I can see a light there. Most often there is total darkness, except on a full moon night. Then, it is so bright you can pick up pebbles on the sandy beach, or look out and see the moon path reflected in the water. Across our valley to the next hill can be seen, just barely now, the roof of the house built by John Matson. The trees and bush are so thick that only parts of the house are visible.

Following the line of the hill and further to the back, are high mountains and deep valleys of trees. No more coconuts trees, except for one standing alone high atop a hill standing tall and proud, silhouetted against the sky. Someone must have carried that plant there a long time ago.

The semi-circle of mountains that surround us are bare except for the *tavioka* (cassava root) plantations that dot the slope. The valley below it at one time produced a thriving rice business for one or two years, helped along by the government. Then it all stopped. Something must have happened. I miss the activity that went along with the rice harvest. From my hill looking down, they seemed like ants scurrying around shouting back and forth. Now all is silent, the bush has taken over and only a carpet of green velvet remains where the rice used to stand. Our yard is shadowed by the patterns of coconut leaves silhouetted against the sun. A coconut falls with a heavy thud on the spot where I stood this morning hanging clothes. It seems imperative now to watch your head. The lemon trees are green and bearing fruit, thanks to all the nocturnal watering from the boys.

Two new water tanks built behind the powerhouse hold our precious water supply. Water is captured from the large expanse of our gull-winged roof into a holding tank. Then it is pumped up to the two large tanks and finally piped back into the house. The drop from the short rise forms enough water pressure for the shower.

From my seat, I can hear the Fijian boys singing in the valley below, whiling away the time as they sell fresh *bu* (green coconut) on the road. They have quite a lucrative market going. It only requires collecting the green coconut and cutting the top off. The liquid is a cool, mildly sweet drink for the thirsty traveler. At fifty cents a drink, it beats a lemonade stand. No sugar to buy or lemons to squeeze.

The clouds are bunching up in the Southwest, piling on top of each other like cotton balls. They will later turn to the dark rain clouds, which keep this side of the island so green and wet. Sitting here on my hill, gazing out at the ocean, I think of the long journey I made as a young wife and mother, all the way from my home in the green hills of Southern Ohio. Never having seen an ocean, or traveled out of my state, or heard of an island called Fiji. Was it bravery or foolhardiness? Would I have started that journey if I could have looked ahead to see what was in store for me? "Yes!" I think to myself. I would not have missed this experience for anything in the world.

Chapter Fifteen

1994

REMEMBERING

Sitting in my favorite chair under the shade of a coconut tree, my mind goes back to the stories of my childhood. I was born in Southern Ohio in a place called Harristation on a hot August night in 1935. My father, Harold Lee Williams, the eldest son in a family of 12, was a farmer who worked hard all his life to provide for his family of six children. I can remember his stories of the hardships of the depression era and what people had to do to survive. Eventually he went to work in the Conservation Corp camps set up by President Roosevelt to help provide work through road and bridge building. From that time on, my father was a Democrat.

Mom, on the other hand, was the only child of a well-to-do, handsome man by the name of Edward H. Rogers, a young black man from a prosperous family. Edward was more at home in tennis whites than work clothes. His liaison with a white woman, Bertie Roamer by name, in the early 1900's in Louisville, Kentucky, resulted in the birth of his only child, my mother, Evelyn Louise. The sight of that brown-skinned child, born out of wedlock in the prevailing racist atmosphere, caused quite a stir. Mom said that she had to be spirited away in the night to keep Bertie's family from killing her as an infant. I do not know the full story. However, the police were involved and the trauma stayed with Mom her whole life. At the sight of a police officer, she would turn the other way, or close her eyes until she was past. It is a pity we do not listen well when stories are told by our parents. We are usually so busy with our own lives. It is not until we get to a reflective age that we remember bits and pieces of what was said.

My grandfather, Edward H. Rogers, once owned a baseball team called the 'Sprudels.' They were the representatives of the mineral water that West Baden Springs, Indiana, was noted for. In those days, trains ran into West Baden, and her sister city, French Lick, Indiana, to partake of the natural mineral water found there. Resort hotels were built around the springs and when bottled, it was shipped all over the world under the name "Sprudel Mineral Water." Grandpa's team belonged to the Negro league. He said that he loved to come into the ballpark and hear hundreds of people rise to their feet and roar with cheers for Grandpa and his team. Now, I wish I had listened more closely to him, too. He used to talk to me in the evening after supper when his 'tonic' had loosened his tongue and refreshed his memory.

He was from a large family. His mother had been run over and killed by a young white boy who had taken his father's car without permission. The boy's parents were prominent in Louisville society, and the headlines read, "Son of Prominent Louisville couple hits and kills "Negress." I thought to myself, that "Negress" was my great-grandmother, mother of twelve children, who washed clothes to hold her family together after the death of her husband. That "Negress" was Mrs. Rogers. She was on her way to work when she was run over and killed by some kid out for a joy ride in his father's car.

All of grandpa's large family were gone by now. Mother his only surviving kin. I was young and sleepy, listening to the ramblings of a tipsy old man. He used to take me with him to Churchill Downs to play the horses. When we came home and walked through downtown Louisville, everyone seemed to know him. They would yell, "Hello, Mr. Rogers! Hi Eddie! How's it going? Good to see you, Eddie." Even the paperboys ran up to talk and get his buck for the paper. Now Eddie must have really had some stories to tell, but all I have are faded photographs of women and men posing in tennis whites, evening gowns and floor length furs next to new Stutz Bearcats and Buick Roadsters.

When Bertie Roamer spirited Mom out of the house, she was only a few day old. In a secret meeting, she gave Mom to Grandpa Rogers. He arranged with an older neighbor woman to look after Mom while he worked. When Mom was 12 years old, Grandpa married Rosetta Stewart. She had a son named Earl. Mom and Uncle Earl grew up together in West Baden Springs, Indiana, where Grandpa spent the last of his working years as the wine steward at the West Baden Springs Hotel.

Mother met my father, Harold Lee Williams from Waverly, Ohio, when he got a job at the same hotel that Grandpa worked at. He rented a room with Grandma and Grandpa Rogers. Before she married, Mom never had to give much thought to anything except whether her shoes and evening gloves matched her evening gown. She was a child used to wealth, summer balls, furs, and kid gloves.

Dad, on the other hand, was a dirt-poor farmer, eldest son of 12 children. His father was also a farmer, Archie

Williams and his wife, Ora Williams. These two people could not have been more different. Dad took Mom to the country in Southern Ohio and left her there during the winters when he returned to West Baden to wait tables to make money since farming did not provide enough for his growing family. Mom was left alone with their three young children, a wood stove, kerosene lights, and loneliness.

Mom loved beautiful nails, having her hair done, and lovely clothes but there was not too much of any of that anymore. I do not think she ever really got the hang of chopping wood, hauling water, and scrubbing clothes on a board, and cold winters. Farmwomen were expected to milk cows, husk corn, and work in the fields beside their husbands. Then they came home to bake bread, trim the lights, wash clothes on a scrubbing board, and do all those things that were part of country living in the early 1930's.

Even though Mom never learned to milk a cow or harness a horse, one thing she took to, with great relish, was canning. I seem to have inherited her love of canning as I can almost do it in my sleep. Mom used to can everything. I distinctly remember us kids picking blackberries and Mom canning 100 quarts of berries one summer. All winter we ate blackberries, in cobbler pies, or dumplings with heavy cream. Sometimes, in the fall, we picked bags and bags of walnuts. Some of them were sold to buy our school clothes. I do not ever remember being hungry, though maybe a little threadbare at times. We were always well fed with a lot of beans, corn bread, dandelion greens, and blackberry cobbler with fresh cream; all still my favorite foods today.

Dad sometimes went to Mackinac Island, Michigan, to supplement his income. I never heard Mom say that she thought she was going to lose her mind with the cold and the kids, or the poverty and the loneliness. I often wondered how I would have managed in that situation with six kids and no husband all through the long, lonely winter months.

Mom never said anything against Dad except one time when we visited the grave of my oldest brother who died of pneumonia at the age of six. Dad must have thought that Mom could not take care of Junior properly because when he got sick with pneumonia, Dad moved him to Grandma Ora William's house against Mom's wishes. Junior died there. Twenty years later, Mom was kneeling by his gravesite and still crying bitter tears thinking that if only she had been allowed to care for her eldest son, he might still be alive.

The highlight of our summer was to drive to West Baden, Indiana, from the farm in Ohio and spend a few weeks in Grandpa's big white house at the top of the hill. Aunt Alice Stewart, Grandma Rosette's mother, lived there with them. Aunt Alice was not a talkative woman but she had a beautiful smile. Not many teeth, but a beautiful smile. She always had candy in her pocket or in her room, and she was always willing to share. She often appeared at our bedroom door just before bedtime, and produced a handful of candy and disappeared back in her room without a word but with a loving smile. We always felt special around her.

In the evening, after dinner Grandpa would set his glass of 'tonic,' which consisted of good old Kentucky bourbon and water, on the piano and belted out a few show tunes for us. For some reason, the only words I can remember is a song that went "Come after breakfast, bring along your lunch, and leave before suppertime." I always thought it was funny. Grandpa was famous for his chicken feet stew. I never tried it, though his dandelion wine and peach brandy were excellent. That I can attest to.

Grandma and Grandpa would review their day late at night in bed and you could always tell when they got to the funny stuff, as Grandma would shout with laughter. One episode that gave her a lot of enjoyment was the time, as she tells it, when she was all dolled up and went downtown in alligator shoes, silk stockings, fur coat and hat. She said she was looking good and really strutting her stuff when she walked across a patch of ice and fell flat on her back. For some reason, that picture always filled her with gales of laughter.

Every summer she would take us children to the store and buy us new clothes. I remember one time she did not have enough cash while shopping, and she sent me out to the car to tell Grandpa to send in some more money. I brought back fifty dollars, she looked at it and told me to go back and tell Grandpa to come into the store and bring his wallet with him.

Grandpa was eventually laid to rest in West Baden. The cemetery was segregated, whites on one side of the road and blacks on the other side. When I went back to visit the grave many years later, I thought Grandpa had the better part of that deal. The few black people who lived in West Baden back then are all buried up high on a round hill with huge granite headstones. These overlook the larger number of white people who are all buried crowded together across the road on the flat area. God always seems to find a way of to even out the odds.

Mom cared for Grandma Rogers after that. Two years to the day that Grandpa Rogers died, Mom took Grandma to the hospital. Grandma was put in the same room that Grandpa had been in. She died at the same hour that Grandpa died, facts that Mom could never quite understand.

Mom loved to dance. All her life, the rhythm of a good band could get her fingers snapping and her toes tapping. When she was younger, I would see her dancing around the room, swinging and swaying to the beat of the music. In later years, her fingers could still snap, her head would sway, and from her wheelchair her feet would tap out the beat.

With Dad, on the other hand, I never saw any music move him. His ear was always glued to the news and the weather reports. Aunt Grace (Sockwell) Daddy's sister, was a beautician, and whenever possible, she would do Mom's hair. Mom had beautiful black hair and when she had just come from the beauty shop she would hold her head in a certain way, very aware of the fact that she was looking good.

With so many children to care for, we did a lot of things to make ends meet, but even then I do not think the ends met a lot of times. Two of my brothers were born with Fragile X Syndrome, a condition that left them unable to speak, arrested mental development and prone to having seizures. The eldest, Harold, Junior, developed pneumonia and died at the age of six, and Robert, my younger brother, developed pancreatic cancer and died at age 32.

One summer, we worked hard cutting and raking hay and hauling it to the barn, my least favorite job on the farm. It was hot, dirty, scratchy work. We had the barn full when, for whatever reason, either lightening or spontaneous combustion, the barn went up in flames. We stood in the yard and watched a whole summer of work go up in smoke. For several days, it was as if someone had died.

Another time, Dad needed to make more money so he got a job as the maintenance man at the Chillicothe Country club. His uncle, Howard White and wife, Aunt Zetta was the caretakers at the club and lived on the grounds. Aunt Zetta took in washing, while Uncle Howard tended the greens. They got Dad the job of cleaning the clubhouse. Dad always took us kids along to help and he would make breakfast for us at the clubhouse. I am not sure if it was something he was supposed to do because one morning we were all sitting around the table eating when the big bosses walked in. They looked at us and we looked at them. I do not know how it went down. We continued to eat our breakfasts at the clubhouse, though we ate somewhat earlier than we did before.

Dad was a very religious man. He tried to teach us about God, about evil ways, and the consequence of falling into sin. He taught us from the Bible about the hellfire that was waiting for us if we were not good.

Mom taught us that there was another world out there beyond the green hills of our home. The strongest swear word Mom ever used was 'damn.' It was not often said and was always preceded by asking for forgiveness for uttering it. In later years, I once made the mistake of taking her to a screening of 'The Color Purple.' The first time the N----- word was said, mother became very indignant. She got up and marched out of the theater. She said it was not nice to use that word.

Mom followed the latest fashion trends, she knew that yellow was in this year, or skirts were going up, or what nail color was in, or the latest dance craze. Not that she could do anything about it, but she followed the trends anyway. Mom and Dad celebrated their 24th wedding anniversary in January 1954. After which, Dad's health began to fail. In July, at the age of 49, he died of cancer. Mom never remarried. She lived on for another 38 years. Over time, Sheila, my younger sister was her companion and caregiver. Mom died peacefully in her sleep under Sheila's watchful care at the age of 86. A week after she died, I heard her whisper in my ear, like the soft fluttering wings of a turtledove. Sometimes, I can hear it still.

We kids encountered a lot of racism at school. We went to Huntington High School and our Principal was a long, tall man named Mr. Lincoln. In earlier years, we were blocked from participating in the plays put on by our classes. His daughter was my teacher and she would read stories to us for an hour in the afternoon. For some reason, she would always pick the stories that contained the "N'.... word. Since I happened to be the only colored student, I took offense to it and one day I told her I did not like what she was doing whereupon she promptly slapped me in the face. I told my father I would not return to school until he took care of things, which he did and in record time. I received an apology and a transfer to another class.

Mr. Harvey Darst took over as principal in my junior year, and it was like the difference between day and night. He made it his business to see that all the kids were treated equally. We were there to learn, not to put up with all that harassment.

One day we got a new school bus driver who told all the colored children, as we got on, to move to the back of the bus. When we got home that night, the parents got an ear full. The next day, instead of the children getting on the bus, all the parents boarded the bus and went en mass to see Mr. Darst. Needless to say, that was the new bus driver's last day at work. We did not fare as well when we decided to attend the white church on our Valley Road. The congregation sent word saying if those N...... kids ever set foot in their church again, they would burn it down. We children said that if they felt that strongly about it, maybe we should not go back. We did not miss much as we did not enjoy the first visit.

~~~~

My thoughts return to Fiji and my seat under the coconut tree, from that long ago time and place in Ohio. Fiji with some three hundred and fifty islands sits like a string of emeralds in the blue waters of the South Pacific. Some are inhabited, some are not. These volcanic islands were ceded to England in 1850 by Ratu Cakobau (pronounced "Thakobau") who was the paramount chief of Fiji at that time. He offered Fiji to the United States but President Lincoln had his hands full with the civil war and said, "No thanks." Ratu Cakobau could not wait until the war was over, as the Germans, and pirates were helping themselves to the island's natural resources of sandalwood and coconuts. Ratu Cakobau had no control over these outsiders, so, Fiji became a British Colony.

The wind is beginning to pick up now, and I feel a few raindrops on my face. The dark clouds are piling up in the southeast. Far out to sea, I can make out the islands of Kadavu, some eighty miles out. The great dome of Mount Washington at one end and a long row of smaller islands are strung out from it. One hundred and fifty miles to the west lay the Yasawa Islands where Richard's grandmother was from. His grandmother's name was Amy. She was called *Bubu*

Amy (Grandmother Amy.) Amy was Ma's (Esther) mother and Amy's brother was named Atunaisa Ralia. He was always just called Momo (Uncle.)

Chapter Sixteen

1960

MOMO

By the time I arrived, Fiji was one hundred years removed from cannibalism.

My cousin, Beverly Gray, a renowned historian in Ohio, has traced our father's side of the family back to the mid-1700's. I quote her now, "An unknown slave woman, who was apparently freed in the mid 1700's, and the 'master's' son had four sons born to them. The mother was free. Therefore, the children were freeborn. The former slave master gave each of his grandson's some land. The names of these men have not yet been clearly established. Allen Cousins, Sr. was the son of one of these four mulatto men". The unknown slave woman was my great, great, great grandmother. As far as I can tell they were honest, hard working, farm people with not a horse thief, or cattle rustler among them.

We cannot say the same about Richard's side of the family where I met my first and only cannibal, Atunaisa Ralia. Yes, Momo was a cannibal. He was Richard's granduncle. When I met Momo, he was nearing one hundred years old. He was a tall, handsome, well-built man, ramrod straight with a permanent twinkle in his eyes. Momo came over one day by boat from the outer islands of the Yasawa to visit with his niece, Esther, Richard's mother. During his visit, he decided to check out the American woman he had heard so much about.

We live on a very steep hill and I thought the climb up the hill would be too much for him and offered to bring the car down to pick him up. Momo would have none of it and came up the hill in first gear and barefoot. Whatever he saw in me he seemed to like, as he came often and sat and talked with me over cups of tea and scones. Momo said he had tasted human flesh when he was a youth. He did not like it and never touched it again. He said he was so old that all of his teeth had fallen out and a new set had grown in. Whether or not that was the case, he had a full set of teeth. Neither did he require glasses to read. One day Momo sailed back to the Yasawas. We all went down to the beach to watch until his boat was out of sight. Momo had made a good friend of this American woman, I was sad to see him go. Though I never saw him again, he has a special place in my heart.

In my mind's eye I can still see Momo standing at the bow of the boat gazing back at the crowd gathered on the beach to see him off. Perhaps, he realized that he would never return to our shores again, and wanting to gather all the memories to himself to take with him to the Yasawas. Much later, Momo's son came to Qaviu to build a boat. When it was finished, he launched it from the same beach that Momo had left from. He called it the "Lady Esther" after Ma.

A few years back, when one of Ma's grandson's, Wallace, Jr., the son of Kini and Wallace, visited Fiji from the US, he took the Blue Lagoon Cruise to the Yasawas. During the dinner cruise from Nadi, a Fijian band serenaded them, and one of the songs was about the boat, the "Lady Esther." Afterwards, when Wallace Jr., told the band boys that the song was about his grandmother, he was taken aside from the tourists and treated like royalty. They held a kava ceremony for him and asked him to stay in the Yasawas for a while so they could take him to visit all of his relatives, descendants of *Bubu* Amy and of *Momo*.

Chapter Seventeen

Pacifica, California May 2005

ONE PERFECT DAY

Our bags are packed now for our summer trip back to Fiji. This year the clan will be gathering for my 70th birthday. It hardly seems possible that forty-five years have passed since I first made that long journey to the South Pacific. But, yes, it has been. Richard and I celebrated our fiftieth wedding anniversary last year in 2004 with over one hundred and twenty family and friends to witness the renewal of our vows. It was what we still call, "One Perfect Day."

The Ram and Williams clan gathered from all over the country and from across the seas. Wallace and Richard's younger brother came from Fiji, Kini was there, and my three sisters, Edna, Sheila, and Rosemarie from Ohio and Indiana. People came from New York, Canada, Fiji, Seattle, Florida, and points in between. We started out with morning Mass at the Good Shepard Church in Pacifica, California. A limousine picked us up at home, courtesy of Shaun and Nathan, Ricky and Cheryl's sons. Diane and Cheryl beautifully decorated the church with some 200 red and white anthiriums flown in from Kauai, Hawaii, by Daisy Nash, one of our dear friends from Fiji. The service was warm and personable, performed by Father Piers Lahey, who said that presiding over marriage renewals was one of his favorite things to do. He had just presided over one ceremony for a couple that had been married for seventy years. Megan, (my grandson Chris's girlfriend) started the readings with "Father, you have made the bonds of marriage a holy mystery, with faith in you and each other they pledge their love today. May their lives always bear witness to the reality of that love." Rebecca, my granddaughter followed with," In the search for God and the good life, in the search for peace and joy, in the search for love among us"…The readings were beautiful. Our vows had to be cut short when Richard was so overcome with emotion; he could no longer continue to speak them. Fred Ross's beautiful singing echoed through the church as we received communion.

Then we were off to the Oyster Point Yacht club, in South San Francisco for an island feast reception. Everyone was so beautiful and handsome. I actually walked past my daughter, Deborah, not recognizing her with her hairdo and dazzling champagne gown. At the reception, Deborah gave a beautiful encapsulation of our fifty years together. Our son, Richard, looking tall and handsome in his dark suit and white shirt, was Master of Ceremonies, making sure that each of the five grandchildren got up and spoke about their "Nana and Bumpa." Richard's brother was sitting with his family, possibly thinking of his own wife Jane, who had passed away two years before. Wallace though suffering from a serious heart condition, asked me for a dance. We danced to a slow waltz; I did not want to tire him. He always loved to dance, often being the first one on the dance floor and the last one off. It was to be our last dance together as he died six months later on Christmas day. His Christmas card to us arrived from Fiji two days after he died.

Ben Work from Canada, Richard's cousin, could hardly contain the tears in his eyes while being among his old friends and relatives again. My younger sister, Rosemarie gave a tearful speech, saying that she could see that "The most important things in life were love and family." Who could forget Christopher, Diane's son, who made a special effort to look nice in his powder blue suit and powder blue shoes to match? Or Kajah, Deborah's son, so comfortable and well spoken in front of a crowd, or Rebecca, Diane's daughter, clicking up to the podium in her two-inch heels and long beautiful legs. Even Nathan, Ricky's son, who hates to speak in front of a crowd even more than I do, did his part, even though his face turned a great shade of red. Shaun, (Ricky's son) is always comfortable in any situation, and Diane, looking as young as her own son and daughter speaking of her love for us. Our former son-in-law, Israel Vila from Florida, Rebecca and Christopher's father, spoke of the bond of love he shared with us for 25 years and how it had not been broken by divorce, or time, or distance. Our dear friends Pam and Satya Deo, who recently celebrated their fifty-five years together, were overjoyed, having the same love and commitment that Richard and I had shared.

The sun was shining beautifully on the white yachts riding at anchor in the San Francisco Bay and the ocean was blue with a slight breeze rippling the surface of the water. Afterwards we cut the cake. A three-tiered masterpiece so beautifully baked and decorated by Cheryl. Cheryl, my dear daughter-in-law had labored over the design and structure for months to get it just right. Fred and his band started up with Richard's and my favorite waltz. My husband looked so elegant in his dark suit, blue and gold shirt, and his distinguished looking, graying hair. He took me into his arms and we danced to Vince Gill's song:

Look At Us

Look at us, after all these years together
Look at us, after all that we've been through
Look at us, still leaning on each other
If you want to see how truelove should be
Then just look at us.

We thought about all the years, the tears, the happiness, the struggles that had brought us to that moment, to that point in our lives, and the happiness we felt to be sharing it with all the people that we love. I can still see the sheer joy on the faces of the 'little ones' as they got to ride home with us in the limo sipping coke from the champagne flutes as we rode along. I do not think they will forget that memory. Arriving at Rick and Cheryl's, we proceeded to rock the house until dawn, everyone dancing and singing, laughing and eating, thoroughly enjoying ourselves and having a great time on a totally, perfect day.

The bags are packed and we are ready to make the journey to Fiji again. At Qaviu, we will take down the storm shutters, remove the dust covers, air out the house, and make up the beds in preparation for the family gathering this summer.

We look forward to new adventures this summer in this house, on this island, in this part of the South Pacific.

Bula Fiji!